Mila

CW00794615

IMMORTALITY OR EXTINCTION?

Is life after death a real possibility? The authors seek to show that this is a substantive question. They criticise philosophers who argue that talk of life after death is unintelligible, and take to task theologians who stipulate that the language of immortality and resurrection refers solely to life here and now.

However, it is one thing to show that talk of life after death is not logical nonsense and that such language essentially refers to some future state. It is quite another to find convincing grounds for such a prospect. And the empirical case for extinction, which depends primarily on the evidence of the natural sciences, is impressive. Moreover the traditional Christian doctrinal framework has become so attenuated as to be unable to supply any substantial support for belief in life after death.

But while 'normal' science points decisively towards extinction certain paranormal data suggest the contrary. The authors pay special attention to 'near-death experiences', as well as considering psychical research and claimed 'memories' of former lives. While they argue that such claimed 'memories' (even if regarded as veridical) are not evidence of personal survival, they find near-death experiences and the best cases provided by psychical research suggestive of continued personal life after death.

The authors find such apparently well-evidenced paranormal data irreconcilable with the implications of normal science, and there seem to be compelling arguments both for and against belief in immortal life. For the religious believer, the balance may be tipped by his experience of a relationship with God which he trusts God will hold in being through death. And although much traditional doctrine has been discarded, this experientially-based hope remains central to Christianity. However for those who doubt the objective reality of the religious dimension, the arguments for extinction may win the day.

Dr Paul Badham is a Lecturer in Theology at St. David's University College, Lampeter, where he teaches modern theology and the philosophy of religion. He studied biblical and patristic theology at Oxford for his initial degree and then taught for one year in a secondary school. At Cambridge he obtained first-class honours in the tripos, part 3, on 'Christian Theology in the Modern World', prior to reading for a PhD at Birmingham. He took up his present appointment in 1973.

Paul Badham is the author of *Christian Beliefs about Life after Death* and has contributed various articles and reviews to *Theology*, *The Expository Times* and other journals.

Dr Linda Badham, his wife, was a research student in the philosophy of science at Lampeter. She graduated with first-class honours in chemistry at the University of Birmingham and taught mathematics and natural science in secondary schools for some years before resuming university work from 1978–81.

LIBRARY OF PHILOSOPHY AND RELIGION

General Editor: John Hick,
H. G. Wood
Professor of Theology, University of Birmingham

This new series of books will explore contemporary religious understandings of man and the universe. The books will be contributions to various aspects of the continuing dialogues between religion and philosophy, between scepticism and faith, and between the different religions and ideologies. The authors will represent a correspondingly wide range of viewpoints. Some of the books in the series will be written for the general educated public and others for a more specialised philosophical or theological readership.

IMMORTALITY OR EXTINCTION?

Paul and Linda Badham
St David's University College
Lampeter, Wales

First published 1982 by
THE MACMILLAN PRESS LTD
London and Basingstoke
Companies and representatives
throughout the world

ISBN 0 333 25933 5

Printed in Hong Kong

Contents

Preface

This book is a collaborative venture by Dr Paul Badham, Lecturer in Theology at St David's University College, Lampeter, and his wife Linda, who was a research student in the philosophy of science at the same college. Paul Badham's interests lie in theology and philosophy of religion and their interaction with the sciences. Dr Linda Badham's initial degree was in chemistry, and her researches in philosophy have been particularly concerned with exploring non-reductionist monistic materialism. As the purpose of this book is to examine a wide variety of arguments for and against life after death, co-operation seemed desirable.

In Part One, we argue that whether or not there can be any life after death is a substantive issue, and that the language of Christian hope has reference to some future state and not primarily to the context of our present earthly life. Part Two is concerned with considerations derived from a naturalistic understanding of the world and man's place in it. We also show that whatever other support a doctrine of a future life may claim, it can no longer rely on the traditional framework of Christian belief. We move on, in Part Three, to consider some paranormal claims which might be taken, at least at face value, as evidential for post-mortem survival. Finally, in Part Four, we try to assess the implications of the arguments adduced in Parts Two and Three.

Every part of this book has been discussed by both of us, and the research and writing of it shared between us. However, where the personal pronoun 'I' has been used to refer to personal experiences or earlier publications, the subject is Paul Badham.

P. B. L. B. *and* L. F. B.

Acknowledgements

I wish to thank Professor Norman Gulley and Dr R. A. Sharpe with whom I have debated the issues of personal identity and survival of bodily death on numerous occasions in our Life after Death seminar in which many of these ideas were hammered out. Additional thanks are due to Dr Sharpe who has also supervised my wife's research in the philosophy of science. Further I am grateful to Professor Carl Lofmark and Rev. Peter Morris for valuable criticisms.

An earlier version of some of the material used in Chapter 5 appeared as 'Death-bed Visions' in *Theology* (July 1980).

I would also like to thank Mrs Margaret Walker for her speedy and accurate typing of the manuscript, and St David's University College for granting me a term's study leave during the writing of this book.

P. B. L. B.

Part One

1 The Logic of Mortality

To many contemporary philosophers life after death is not merely unlikely, it is inconceivable. It is not a question of weighing the evidence and finding it wanting, but rather of analysing the language and finding it meaningless. If a person claimed to be able to draw a square circle, we would feel no obligation to look at his work before returning a negative judgement upon it; simply to know the meaning of the words 'square' and 'circle' is to know that his project is doomed. In like manner it is suggested that if we pay attention to the correct usage of words relating to personal identity we will recognise that talk of 'persons surviving bodily death' is literally nonsense.

Antony Flew is one powerful advocate of this position for which he has coined the slogan, 'people are what you meet'.[1] And what we meet are creatures of flesh and blood who can be pointed at, touched, heard, seen and talked to. It is to such beings that words like 'you', 'I', or 'he' relate. 'Person words refer to people. And how can such objects as people survive physical dissolution?'.[2] Moreover consider how we use the word 'survive': it always relates to those who come through situations of danger, and in fact 'we so use the word "survive" that it is logically impossible for one and the same passenger to be after a crash both dead and a survivor'.[3] Flew's argument can be usefully supplemented by consulting a dictionary. No one would question that 'the living body of a human being' does not survive the flames of the crematorium, nor that 'the functional activity of the organised matter constituting the human animal' ceases to operate in the corrupting corpse. Yet the phrases quoted are meanings given by the Concise Oxford Dictionary to the words 'person' and 'life', so how can such words be seriously thought to be usable in a supposed after death situation? And this difficulty is heightened when we note that according to the same dictionary 'to die' means 'to cease to live, to lose vital force, to decay, come to an end, cease to exist, be forgotten, or fade away'. So whether we focus on the words associated with 'life' or 'death', we have to

3

acknowledge that they apply in mutually incompatible contexts as 'opposites' to one another. Consequently by the law of logic known as 'the principle of the excluded middle' we seem forced to conclude that where one is present the other is not. So if an entity is correctly described as 'dead' it is logically invalid to describe that same entity as also 'alive'.

Wittgenstein has shown that a primary source of philosophical confusion is the popular tendency to ignore the everyday use of the language we speak, and the context in which we learnt to utter the phrases we use. His influence has been especially marked in the philosophy of mind where a generation of able scholars has sought to track the language of selfhood to its source in the everyday relationships of family and social life.[4] It is easy to show that we initially learn the use of words like 'I', 'self' and 'person' by reference to living embodied creatures of flesh and blood, and we discover the meaning of the word 'death' by observing the evidence of corruption and decay in once living plants or animals. So it is argued that we ought to recognise that talk of a future life could be held to exemplify the logical confusion which can follow when 'language goes on holiday'.[5] Wittgenstein's own position is that if we pay attention to the meaning of the words involved we will realise that 'death is not lived through' and that 'the world in death does not change, but ceases'.[6]

It is as well that we commence our inquiry into the future hope by facing squarely the 'no entry' sign which common language erects across the road to immortality. For common language reflects common experience, and there is nothing that experience teaches so firmly and so decisively than that 'all men are mortal', so that this expression itself has become the standard example of a logical truism. And no facile claim that 'death does not exist'[7] can begin to do justice to the reality of the human situation, or honestly take note of that horizon which, humanly speaking, 'seals off the future' for us.[8]

A Christian theologian might be expected to draw the teeth of the linquistic opposition by expounding the ancient doctrine of the Resurrection of the Body. The Apostles' Creed in the original Latin, unmistakably affirms a belief that 'the flesh' which perishes will one day be 'raised up' (*resurrectio carnis*), and the Nicene Creed equally bluntly looks forward to 'the up-standing of the corpses' (*anastasin nekron*). According to a recent Catholic *Catechism for Adults* this means that each person will one day rise again 'as the same person he was, in the same flesh made living by the same spirit'.[9] Such a robust faith need fear no attack from the logician for the resurrected body would, by definition, meet all our present criteria for personal identity and physical aliveness. If every single particle of which our bodies were composed at the moment of death were to be gathered together by divine omnipotence, and if we were all restored to the same condition that we were in before our final illness,[10] then in almost every sense of the word 'we' would live again.

But I cannot take this route, for although the doctrine of fleshly resurrection can withstand the onslaughts of linguistic analysis, I believe it has to surrender to objections from other quarters. Modern biology teaches us that our bodies are not composed of distinctive particles which belong to us permanently, but rather are made up of constantly changing living cells which form part of an ongoing cycle of life. Moreover many today die of old age after years of progressive weakness and decline and so would not want 'the identical structure which death had destroyed'[11] to be restored. In earlier ages when most were struck down in youth or middle life by sudden illness, it seemed feasible to think of restoration to the full health enjoyed earlier. It is harder to think in such terms when perhaps a decade or more of increasing decrepitude may have preceded the final illness.

A greater difficulty is that a reconstituted human being could only live on earth, or a planet of some other star with the same sort of biosphere as earth. The sheer number of human beings already born and yet to come would require thousands of such planets to be colonised. Such planets would have to evolve with all the necessary vegetable and animal life to sustain man, but with no indigenous competitor for our ecological niche. And all this would have to happen so that one day these other planets would be able to receive resurrected earthmen who would arrive out of the blue at adulthood to take up residence upon them. The further one explores the implications of all this the more bizarre it all seems.[12] Such practical considerations cannot be avoided by saying that the resurrected bodies would be wholly transformed and suited for a new life in heaven. For any such transformation would re-open the door to the linguistic objections which face all other doctrines of a future life, i.e. in what sense could a 'wholly transformed body suited for a new life in heaven' be considered to be 'the same body' as that which was laid in the tomb?

The point I am making is that, of all possible doctrines of a future life, only the doctrine of the resurrection of this flesh, taken in a totally literal and unsophisticated sense, can avoid the challenge of contemporary philosophers about its meaningfulness as a possible future destiny for flesh and blood creatures like ourselves. Yet almost all Christians today would endorse John Macquarrie's judgement that even if the resurrection or the re-creation of our present embodiment is thought to lie within the bounds of possibility, 'it is such a remote and even bizarre possibility, that it is hard to see that it offers much support for belief in a life to come'.[13] Consequently I believe that any viable concept of a future life has to talk in terms, either of the immortality of the soul, or of a resurrection which does not entail the resuscitation or re-creation of our present bodies.

But in what sense could either destiny be regarded as a continuation of my present selfhood? An invisible, intangible, disembodied soul is a very different sort of entity from an embodied creature of flesh and blood, so why should we suppose that the same personal pronoun can be applied to both?[14] Yet unless the soul that lives on is 'me' the supposed immortality of this unobservable entity is of no conceivable interest. Likewise if God created a 'spiritual body' suited for a wholly new kind of life in a resurrection world, why should we suppose that this new creation could be regarded as the same person as the one who died? Yet unless it is the same person, its creation would be of no more vital concern to us than the existence of whatever life forms we may suppose to have evolved on the eight hundred million other planets in our galaxy which may be suitable locations for the emergence of intelligent life. Life after death depends on the continuation or restoration of the person who existed before death. This alone is what gives doctrines of immortality their huge human interest.[15]

Consequently life after death can only be a meaningful concept if it is possible to show that there is a legitimate sense in which 'person language' can be extended beyond its normal usage to relate either to an immaterial soul, or to a 'spiritual body' newly created by divine omnipotence. The problem is, as Flew rightly observes, that 'person words are quite manifestly and undeniably taught and learnt and used by and for reference to a certain sort or corporeal object.'[16] But why should this fact be supposed to veto any extension of the meaning of these words? Flew's argument depends on the quite groundless assumption that the meaning of words is irrevocably shaped by the environment in which we first learnt how to use them. Yet as even Sir Alfred Ayer, the doyen of linguistic philosophers, points out, there is 'no reason why the meaning of words should be indissolubly tied to the contexts in which they are originally learnt'.[17] And with regard to most words in our vocabulary no one would dream of making such an assumption. Consider the word 'sun'. It would seem that the word 'sun' is 'quite manifestly and undeniably taught and learnt and used by and for reference' to a circle of warming light which we observe rising in the east, moving across the sky during the day, and sinking below the horizon in the west. Yet since Copernicus and Galileo we have learnt to modify and extend our usage and understanding of 'sun-talk' in the light of further knowledge and experience. Moreover we find that concept modification occurs across the whole range of scientific advance, so that it is almost axiomatic that the acquisition of new knowledge seems to entail the extension, if not the contradiction of the initial understanding of language which we were taught in childhood.[18]

We ought not therefore to rule out even the possibility that as our knowledge and understanding of what it means to be a person grows and develops, we may wish to extend and modify our initial understanding of person words. And this is especially true of our usage of the personal pronoun 'I'. Flew lists all person words together and asserts that words like ' "you", "I", "person", "Flew", "woman", "father", "butcher" all refer in one way or another to objects'.[19] I do not think I am making a purely grammatical point by remarking that the word 'I' can never be so used, but must always relate to the subject. This is in part a verbal quibble reflecting the fact that pronouns have kept both nominative and accusative forms, but there may be more to it than this. For there is a real difference between our subjective experience of our own self-hood and our objective experience of the individuality of others.

It is true of course that we first learn how to use the word 'I' by observing the public behaviour of other people, and this includes noting their usage of the personal pronoun in connection with their private thoughts and feelings. Language used to denote private emotional states and feelings can be learnt, because people normally tell the truth and we are therefore able to associate observable patterns of behaviour with reported private experiences. Thus we learn how to use the language of intentionality by observing that declared intentions are normally translated into the actions predicted. And we learn the language of feeling by noticing that cries of anguish and tears are associated with talk of being in pain, while expressions of pleasure and radiant smiles are accompanied by claims to feel happy. However, having once learnt the meaning of words like 'pain' and 'happy' by reference to outward behaviour, there is nothing to prevent us subsequently using the words to refer primarily to the inner feelings which normally give rise to such behaviour.[20]

Moreover since our inner feelings do not necessarily have to find expression in outward behaviour, it is quite possible for us to act in such a way that no one could ever discover what we are really thinking. Consider the following sentences: 'I intend to mow the lawn this evening'; 'I feel a slight pain'; 'When I close my eyes I see a yellow after–image'; 'I dreamt I was in China'. All these statements should be perfectly meaningful to anyone who has learnt how to use the English language. Yet the accuracy of such reports can be known only to the person who makes them. Tests of verification or falsification are inadequate to cope with reports of private thoughts and feelings. Thus my intention to mow the lawn this evening could be genuine even if a downpour of rain frustrated its fulfilment, and my slight pain could have been masked from others by a stoic cheerfulness if I had not chosen to speak about it. I might have lied about seeing a yellow after–image in order not to be left out of philosophical discussions in which these unusual experiences are so often talked about,[21] and a person who talks of dreaming about China might simply be using this as a device to introduce the subject of his visit there into a conversation.

What I really think, feel, intend, inwardly experience, or dream is always inaccessible to others unless I choose by word or deed to reveal it to them. Yet my thoughts, feelings and intentions are of the utmost importance to me. Indeed for the individual, self-identity is constituted far more fundamentally by his thoughts, feelings and intentions than by his physical embodiment or by his situation in space and time. Consider the claim some people make to have dreams in which the subject of the dream experiences has (or is) another body, answers to another name, and exists in a different historical context from the dreamer. The dreamer will nevertheless identify himself with the subject of those dream experiences.

For a person to utter the words, 'I dreamt I was Napoleon', implies that subjectively he does not identify his self-hood as intrinsically or necessarily bound up with his present physical embodiment, name, or situation in time and space. Otherwise he could not have dreamed that he was Napoleon. Bernard Williams argues that to imagine oneself as Napoleon is in practice no more than to imagine oneself in the role of Napoleon.[22] This would seem correct in that the dreamer always considers his dream experience to be continuous with his own mental life, so that while he may take over the name, role and situation of Napoleon he preserves his own conscious awareness.

However, I disagree with Williams' further suggestion that one could give a straightforwardly third person account of all this and say that someone had a dream in which he acted the role of Napolean just as Charles Boyer played the part of the French Emperor in a film. The question is 'which "self" plays the role?'. Let us suppose that I suffer from the *folie de grandeur* we are discussing. It would not be a case of my dreaming that 'I, the publicly identifiable Paul Badham, was playing the role of Napoleon as Charles Boyer did in the film', but rather that in my dream, 'I, the subject of my conscious experiences, found myself in a Napoleon – like body and a Napoleon – like historical situation answering to the name of the French Emperor, and having a variety of adventures which probably owed more to my memories of Tolstoy's *War and Peace* than to any serious historical context'.

The point of this digression is that if it is essential to the meaning of the personal pronoun 'I' that I use it to relate to Paul Badham, a particular physical being living in a particular historical setting, then it would seem impossible even in a dream for me to identify myself with another and different embodiment and historical situation. But if we concede that in imagination, or dream, I can identify my selfhood with another name, body, and life-style, then it ceases to be meaningless to envisage the possibility that I could also identify my selfhood with another and different embodiment after death. I could still be 'I' though clothed with a new and different body, provided only that this new body was suitable as a vehicle for the expression of my distinctive thoughts, feelings and self–awareness.

In support of this claim let us note that few seem to find any difficulty at all in following the plots of fairy tales and of science fiction stories which involve body transfer. If the meaning of self were identical with the meaning of body, this would be impossible and such stories would simply be unintelligible. Antony Flew suggests that talk of minds moving from one body to another is still regarded as acceptable because of the continued dominance of Platonic–Cartesian assumptions in our society,[23] but this I cannot believe. The children who sit enthralled watching Dr Who or Star Trek have never heard of either Plato or Descartes, and if asked would almost certainly identify their minds with their brains.[24] 'He's brainy', or 'he's got a brain like a computer' are the present ways of describing high intelligence. If contemporary children are prepared to accept at least the intelligibility of body transfer it is in spite of, not because of, their assumptions about the way we think. As Flew correctly observes the word soul 'is little used on weekdays'[25] and on Sundays few modern children come within range of such discourse.

I suggest that the reason why talk of body transfer is generally felt to be intelligible is that personal identity is discerned in two very different ways. We identify the personality of others through their distinctive physical characteristics and behavioural patterns. And this in turn is how they normally recognise us. But we do not recognise ourselves through observation but through our inner feelings. What makes me 'me' is not my external appearance, to which I may be relatively indifferent, or even my characteristic behavioural patterns of which others may be more conscious than myself. But rather it is that I am the subject of the thoughts, feelings, memories and intentions of which I am aware.[26]

Imagine that tomorrow morning I woke up feeling the same as usual, remembering what had happened today and thinking about my plans for that day as for any other. Then let us suppose that on looking into the bathroom mirror, I discovered that the face which I proposed to shave was completely unfamiliar to me. If this happened, I would undoubtedly be terrified, bewildered and utterly distraught, but I could not doubt my own identity if my thinking remained the same. In the end, I would be forced to conclude that *I* had by some means acquired a new and different body. I would have no choice about arriving at this conclusion for what would it be to doubt that one was the person one was conscious of being?[27]

Two possible replies to this argument spring to mind. Bernard Williams suggests that the situation could be best explained by saying that the person looking into the mirror had 'misremembered what he looked like'.[28] It was for this reason that I talked of a '*completely* unfamiliar face', and of a shaving mirror. One can indeed sometimes be surprised at catching a reflection of oneself in a full length mirror or seeing one's profile from an unfamiliar angle. But could one really misremember the part of one's face one shaves every day? However, even if Williams' interpretation of the data were to be accepted, it would itself provide a striking argument for identifying selfhood with one's own mental experiences, rather than one's external characteristics. So on either interpretation the story supports my thesis.

The second reply to this story argues that in using the word 'I' for the subject of the experience of looking in the mirror at an unfamiliar face I have begged the question at issue. However this is no problem, for we can quite easily retell the story in terms of a person waking up with thoughts and feelings identical to those Mr X had had on the previous day, and then looking in the mirror at a face wholly unlike the face of Mr X. Even in this case however I suggest this anonymous person with Mr X's thoughts and feelings, but without Mr X's body, would still identify himself as the person he was conscious of being although in an unfamiliar body. Would any alternative really be open to a person who found himself in this bizarre position?[29]

But is talk of a person obtaining a new body the right way to describe the situation? Bernard Williams has attempted an ingenious and very influential rebuttal of all stories purporting to support body transfer. He asks us to imagine a person being told that tomorrow he would be tortured, but before being tortured all his memories would be removed, and in their place he would be fed with impressions of a past life extracted from the brain of another person.[30] Williams suggests that this would compound the horror of the impending torture. He then argues that his schema is no more than another way of describing an example of a body transfer case. In body transfer terms, Person A is told that tomorrow his body will be tortured, but before that happens he will exchange bodies with Person B so that it is Person B who will experience the pain of torment.

But I suggest the two cases are not comparable. Memories alone do not constitute self-identity. However, if my memories, self-awareness, thought-processes and feelings were all taken away from my body I would not mind what happens to it. The flames of the crematorium will not torture 'me' for 'I' shall not be there. Either I will cease to exist with my body or I shall continue to exist without it. Returning to Williams' story and amending it to refer to the whole of my mental life being removed from my body and the whole of another person's mental life being incorporated into it, I would argue that if my former body were then tortured, I would feel sorry for its new occupant, and would be distressed at the desecration of my re-animated corpse but would feel no personal fear, for the torture as such would not affect 'me'. Consequently I do not think Williams' argument affects the thesis I have been presenting that the personal pronoun 'I' relates primarily to 'the subject of my conscious experiences'.

My argument is that thinking, feeling and self-awareness constitute the sense of individuality each person possesses. It may be that as a matter of empirical fact this self-awareness is contingently dependent on my present physical state, and this is something we must explore in a later chapter. But our present concern is solely with the question of whether talk of personal survival of bodily death is an intelligible concept or a meaningless paradox. And my claim is that if we examine the way the word 'I' comes to be used in the experience of dreaming, and in our sense of what constitutes personal identity for the individual subject, then we can say that talk of personal life after death may indeed be meaningful. If it is intelligible to identify the self with a different embodiment and a different historical setting in a dream or in a story, then it is intelligible to identify the self with a different embodiment and a different setting in a life after death. Hence although at this stage in the argument we may regard the acquisition of a new 'spiritual body' for life in a resurrection world as an unlikely event, I do not think we can dismiss it as literally nonsense in the way that writers like Bernard Williams and Antony Flew urge us to do.

Let us now turn to the question of whether or not it is intelligible to consider the possibility of us surviving death in a wholly disembodied state. Here I think we need to consider carefully reports from people who have been resuscitated in intensive care units who would undoubtedly have died but for prompt medical attention. Many such patients have claimed that at the moment of apparent death they found themselves out-of-their-bodies, looking down from above at the resuscitation attempts. We shall explore the possible evidential status of such claims in chapter five. For the present let us simply note that these experiences are widely described, discussed and generally found to be intelligible in the sense that people seem able to understand the claims being made even if they differ on how such experiences are to be interpreted. Antony Flew describes the situation thus: 'It has seemed to the subjects as if they were observing themselves from a point of view outside themselves', and he goes on to assert 'whatever explanation is to be offered for these curious experiences they surely have no tendency to show that a person word must be used to refer to an incorporeal entity which might significantly be said to detach itself from the person in question'.[31]

Flew has been able to arrive at this conclusion by altering one key element in the evidence. He talks of the patients observing from a point of view 'outside themselves'. In fact however this is not the claim made. Rather those who have this experience always talk of being 'outside their bodies'. They identify their self-hood with the subject of the experience of being out-of-the-body and of looking down with interest on the resuscitation attempts. Hence Flew's conclusion does not follow and the evidence, which as long ago as 1965 he acknowledged to be based on 'a fair number . . . of reliable claims', does indicate a widespread use of person words to refer to an incorporeal entity which may significantly be said to detach itself from the body in question.

The point is that the people who have this experience do use person words in this way. They claim that they actually did go out of their bodies and observed what was going on in the ward from a different point. And since there is at least some evidence that their observations were correct, and were consistent with 'seeing' from above, rather than from the position of the body on the operating table, a *prima facie* case exists for considering the explanation they give seriously. Flew insists that because we know what it is to be a person we must assimilate such experiences to imagination and say that out-of-the-body experiences are simply the product of the imagination of the patient who lies 'in his bed apparently unconscious'.[32] This seems a very dangerous argument to use. It is in fact almost identical to the one used by the Cardinals opposed to Galileo, who refused to take seriously his claims to have observed moons circling Jupiter on the grounds that they knew the principles of astronomy on which the solar system operated and hence any alleged new data must be the product of Galileo's imagination.

The lesson of the Galileo incident is that neither philosophers nor theologians should seek to pre-empt the findings of empirical research about the nature of man or the universe on the basis of a preconceived theory of what is or is not possible. Many people believe that the claim to observe from a point of view other than that of the body is a straightforwardly empirical claim which could be settled one way or another by careful analysis of the correctness or otherwise of the claimed observations. I shall argue in chapter five that the issue is not quite as straightforward as that, but I accept the basic assumption behind this claim that the status of out-of-the-body experiences involves empirical evidence as well as philosophical analysis.

In short I believe that whether or not I can have experiences outside my body is a factual issue, and one for which the evidence of alleged out-of-the-body experiences is crucial. I would also claim that if it is possible to present good grounds for believing that consciousness can function apart from the body before death, then it is intelligible to argue that consciousness might function apart from the body after death. And if my earlier argument for equating consciousness with the self is valid, then 'I' could survive bodily death.

It must however be acknowledged that both the word 'I' and the word 'survive' are not being given their normal meanings when we talk of survival of death. For immortality lies outside the frontiers of everyday speech, which has evolved as a means of communication between living, embodied human beings in the context of their common life in this world. Under normal circumstances at least there is no communication between the living and the departed.[33] Hence as the Funeral Psalm puts it, at death 'we bring our years to an end as it were a tale that is told'.[34] After my heart has stopped beating for the last time the publicly identifiable Paul Badham will be no more, and any language used about him as a person would have to move into the past tense. Consequently it is inevitable and inescapable that the language of death should be opposed to the language of life. No matter how firmly we may believe in a future existence, it is simply a fact that when a person dies he ceases to belong to that shared context of experience with which our common language is concerned.

The most influential exponents of immortality have always recognised this. Thus the elders at Miletus wept when they realised that St Paul was going to his death and that consequently they would see his face no more.[35] And Plato recognised that the pathos of the death-cell conversation he reported in the *Phaedo* came about because all present were aware that this would be the last time that Socrates and his friends would be able to talk together.[36]

The Requiem Mass speaks of 'heartening with the promise of immortality to come those of us who are saddened by the certainty of dying'.[37] There is no evasion here. Both the sorrow, and the inescapable character of death are fully acknowledged. And yet the

Requiem goes on to talk of life being 'changed not ended'. Any such change would of necessity be profound. Yet the argument of this chapter is that if we pay attention to the way each individual recognises his own identity in this present life it is not a meaningless suggestion that we could envisage the possibility of individual continuity even through such a change. And even if some still feel that the word 'person' ought not to be used outside its present reference to physically embodied creatures, this need not be a stumbling block in the way of an immortal hope. As R. H. Thouless argues, 'the essential issue about survival is not as to what happens to the human personality (the self as met by other people) but as to what happens to the stream of consciousness. This is of course directly verifiable only by the individual himself, and by him only after the death of his body'.[38] Sir Alfred Ayer makes the same point 'if there could conceivably be disembodied spirits, the fact that it would not be correct to call them persons would not perhaps be of very great importance'.[39] The one irreducible minimum for talk of life after death is that in some sense 'I' could still be 'I' after the permanent death of my present body. Examination of the way we use the language of our own self-hood keeps that possibility open for us.

Finally, let me stress that in arguing for the use of 'person' words in cases which must be viewed as extensions from the usual contexts of correct application, I am not advocating the view of Lewis Caroll's Humpty Dumpty: ' "When *I* use a word" Humpty Dumpty said in a rather scornful tone, "it means just what I choose it to mean–neither more nor less" '.[40] My point is only that words are not irrevocably and immutably determined by their original usage. But change has to be agreed by a significant proportion of the language-using community. It cannot be at the mere stipulation of one or a few individuals or there will be a break-down in communication. Moreover, when a new stipulated usage is suggested by its proponent(s) to be the 'real' meaning of that term in earlier writers we have double grounds for complaint: first that this is not agreed usage and secondly that to apply it retrospectively is to distort the message of an earlier writer. It is one thing to argue that one believes some author to be in error; it is quite another to change the content of what he says so as to make it fit one's own beliefs. Yet that is what has happened in much twentieth century theological and philo-sophical writing on the themes of resurrection, immortality and eternal life. It is to these unfortunate efforts that we now turn.

2 The Meaning of Resurrection, Immortality and Eternal Life

The philosophical problems we discussed in the last chapter, combined with the empirical difficulties we shall consider in the next, have led many Christian theologians to the conclusion that life after death is no longer a tenable belief. Gordon Kaufman is one of the most explicit, 'individuals die in a matter of a few years and we have no reason to suppose that their life continues beyond the grave'.[1] And Kaufman insists that he holds this view as a Christian scholar consciously working within the framework of faith. Schubert Ogden also defends the appropriateness of such a position: 'What I must refuse to accept, precisely as a Christian theologian, is that belief in our subjective existence after death is in some way a necessary article of Christian belief'.[2]

However, many Christians would find such a conclusion very difficult to justify. For Christianity is a historical religion, based on a supposedly divine revelation, which has been developed through the centuries in a continuous tradition, and which has found expression in forms of worship and prayer which continue to nourish the Christian life. And it is easy to show that the doctrine of resurrection is the focal point of the New Testament,[3] that belief in eternal life lies at the heart of Christian sacramental teaching,[4] and that the hope of immortality has done more to sustain the faith of the ordinary Christian believer than any other doctrine.[5]

Consequently theologians who identify themselves strongly with the life of the Church find it very hard simply to discard language which is as deeply rooted in the Christian consciousness as is talk of 'the resurrection of the dead, and the life of the world to come'.[6] And their difficulties are often compounded by the fact that they are called upon professionally to teach and interpret documents and formularies in which such language occurs, or to conduct services whose phraseology is redolent with such doctrines.

Rudolf Bultmann illustrates this dilemma very well. He is convinced that 'resurrection from the dead is utterly inconceivable'. It could never be established as remotely possible 'no matter how many witnesses are cited'.[7] And Bultmann's total rejection of resurrection extends not only to the literal concept of the resuscitation of the corpse, but also to the more sophisticated notion of the 'clothing of the human personality . . . with a spiritual body', which he describes as 'not only irrational but completely meaningless'.[8] Yet Bultmann was a Lutheran pastor as well as a university professor, and most of his students were seeking ordination into a church in which they would be expected to proclaim the resurrection faith of Christendom. And clearly this raised problems, as Bultmann himself was well aware: 'Convinced as I am that a corpse cannot come back to life and rise from his tomb . . . what am I to do when as a pastor, preaching or teaching I must explain texts? . . . or when as a scientific theologian, I must give guidance to pastors with my interpretation?'.[9] Bultmann's solution to his problem is not to renounce his allegiance to the resurrection faith, but instead to re-interpret that faith so that henceforth it should be understood as having an entirely secular connotation. Consequently although Bultmann continues to use the language of resurrection and of the Easter faith, in his usage it no longer relates either to the historical Jesus or to the future destiny of man, but instead refers to our present experience in the here and now. This technique has been followed by many other Christian writers with the consequence that as Antony Flew puts it, beliefs 'which actually started out as doctrines of personal immortality have been so interpreted by philosophers and theologians that they have surreptitiously ceased to be anything of the kind'.[10] This technique is described by W. Lippmann as 'that weasel method of sucking the meaning out of words, and then presenting the empty shells in an attempt to palm them off as giving the Christian Faith a new and another interpretation'.[11]

The terms 'resurrection', 'immortality', 'eternal life' and 'future hope' have been particularly vulnerable to such methods of interpretation so that before proceeding to use such terminology in my own investigation of the possibility of life after death I must first seek to establish that that really is the context to which such terms belong.

Let us start with the language of resurrection. We have already noted that Rudolf Bultmann severs all connection between such language and the ultimate fate of the historical Jesus or ourselves. Like Harry Williams he believes that talk of resurrection is not 'about what can be held to have happened in the environs of Jerusalem and Galilee on the third day after Jesus was crucified or about what can be held to be in store for us after our own death'.[12] Instead such language should be seen as referring to the quality of our present existence. Several other writers take this line. Thus H. J. Richards denies that 'the resurrection of the body is a guaranteed future bonus' rather it is 'a present reality';[13] Nicholas Lash argues that 'belief in resurrection is compatible with disbelief in life "after death" ';[14] and Jurgen Moltmann even claims that 'resurrection of the dead excludes any idea of a life after death'.[15]

The reason this kind of interpretation appears possible, is that the New Testament places considerable weight on the existential consequences of belief in the resurrection of Christ, and that St Paul often uses the imagery of resurrection to describe the new quality of life which should be present in the believer through the power of the indwelling and risen Christ.[16] St Paul also draws a direct analogy between the literal death and resurrection of Jesus and the metaphorical death to sin, and rising up to righteousness which should follow incorporation into Christ in baptism: 'in the same way you must regard yourselves as dead to sin and alive to God in union with Christ Jesus'.[17]

However Paul is able to use the language of resurrection in a metaphorical sense only because in the resurrection of Jesus he supposes it to have a factual meaning. And neither St Paul's stress on the existential consequences of belief, nor his metaphorical use of resurrection language to refer to moral reform, should be allowed to blur the fact that for St Paul the primary use of resurrection language is to refer to new life after physical death in the case either of Jesus, or of the Christian believer. The discussion in 1 Corinthians 15 would be meaningless except on such a supposition, and it is especially relevant to note that in verse 19 St Paul explicitly declares that 'if it is for this life only that Christ has given us hope, we of all men are most to be pitied'. In the letter to the Phillipians Paul does indeed state that he hopes to know the power of Christ's resurrection in his present life, but he also makes it plain that his own resurrection would involve a departure from his present body, that 'to die is gain', and that his true citizenship is in heaven.[18] Likewise, although St Paul talks, in the second letter to the Corinthians, of the present indwelling power of Christ's spirit, he twice explicitly describes this as 'a pledge of what is to come'.[19] There seems therefore no doubt that for St Paul the resurrection always entails a future hope which is to be realised only after the death of our present bodies.[20]

It is true that some early Christians must have supposed that talk of the resurrection related to this present life, for in the second letter to Timothy we read that some were teaching that the resurrection had already happened. But what is most significant is that either Paul himself, or the disciple of Paul who may have written this letter, wholly repudiates such teaching as 'empty and worldly chatter' which 'will spread like a gangrene' leading those who indulge in it 'further and further into godless courses'.[21]

It is therefore hard to see how such teaching can be legitimately revived in our day as an interpretation of Pauline thought. This is not to espouse any kind of biblical fundamentalism. Any modern Christian must feel free to challenge biblical teaching which he believes to be mistaken. What is not justifiable however is to interpret a passage as meaning something which the author himself explicitly repudiated as being his meaning. And even if the witness of 2 Timothy is disregarded, we have sufficient evidence in the other data we have considered to be sure that Paul would wholly reject any secular interpretation of the resurrection hope.

However let us temporarily suspend the objection that talk of the resurrection as a present reality does not fully do justice to St Paul's usage, and let us consider only the question of whether or not it is intelligible. According to H. A. Williams 'resurrection' can be seen whenever we realise anew our full potential as human beings. When, after a long run of mediocre tennis playing I play a really good game, there is resurrection; or when a young man jaded by a long run of sexual affairs falls deeply in love; or an elderly widow rediscovers the value of physical contact, there too in resurrection.[22] One question which immediately springs to mind is, 'why should anyone use the word "resurrection" to describe such experiences?'. It does not seem a particularly appropriate word, and it is certainly not normally used in such contexts. I have never heard a Wimbledon commentator talk of a player's 'resurrection', and if he did would it be thought of as anything more than a rather bizarre metaphor?

Let us consider Williams' example of the promiscuous young man in more detail. In the story we are told that one of the many girls the young man sleeps with is a typist at his office to whom he is

physically 'more than usually attracted'. With her he discovers a
new depth in his sexual feelings and so they marry and when in the
marriage service the young man said to his bride ' "with my body I
thee worship" it was a statement of literal fact'. Williams comments,
'Here . . . if anywhere . . . we see . . . the resurrection of the flesh.
The dead body . . . raised up to a new life of glory'.[23] Frankly I
believe most people would regard the use of the term 'resurrection'
in such a context as a crude joke. It is hard to believe that a member
of the Community of the Resurrection could give so banal an
interpretation of the term.

My reason for spelling out this example in full is that it happens
precisely to contradict Bultmann's interpretation of what resurrection life entails. According to Bultmann, rising to the new way of life
means the 'crucifying of the affections and lusts of the flesh', 'casting
off the works of darkness' and enjoying 'a freedom, albeit a
struggling freedom from sin'. It also includes 'the overcoming of our
dread of suffering, and the perfection of our detachment from the
world'.[24] It would be hard to imagine two more different interpre-
tations of the alleged meaning in everyday life of the term
'resurrection'; unless perhaps we go on to compare Bultmann's
usage with that of Moltmann.

According to Moltmann 'resurrection from the dead' means 'a
wholehearted, unrestricted and unreserved assent to life, to the
body and to the world',[25] and manifests itself in social and political
concern and action to achieve righteousness in human history.[26]
Such an understanding seems very far removed from 'perfecting our
detachment from the world'! We are offered another type of
explanation by H. J. Richards who thinks that the resurrection
body which is so central to the Christian's hope is in fact 'nothing
other than the Church'.[27] We rise from the dead when we join the
Christian community. And Nicholas Lash gives yet another
interpretation. For him the risen life is a way of looking at our
present life as if from the standpoint of God's eternity. Resurrection
life is thus our present life 'as experienced by us from the standpoint
of God'.[28] Just how we are to get this standpoint is not made clear,
but it is in no sense 'another mode of existence' for Lash believes
there is only one 'single historical process' and that is the one in
which we now live.

This analysis of various proposals for new uses for the word
'resurrection' suggests that when the word is cut loose from its
central mooring, as a term referring to life after death, it ceases to

have any real meaning. Consequently each of the five theologians I have mentioned is able to put forward his own idiosyncratic usage. But since language is only meaningful when there is at least some agreement over its use, talk of 'resurrection' tends to become vacuous when it is taken to relate solely to our present existence. What then does 'resurrection' mean? The English word is simply a transliteration of the Latin for 'rising again', and corresponds to the Greek anastasis which means 'standing up'. Hence Bultmann is right in saying that the literal meaning of resurrection is of a corpse rising up to life anew. And this usage seems confirmed when we study the reports in the Gospels relating to Jesus' appearances. We find talk of Jesus having risen from the dead, being juxtaposed to talk of the place where they had laid him, and of the tomb being empty and the grave clothes scattered.[29] We hear of Mary Magdalene being asked to stop clinging to Jesus, and of Thomas being invited to touch him.[30] We find explicit mention of Jesus' risen body possessing 'flesh and bones', and we are told that his disciples 'ate and drank with him after he rose from the dead'.[31] Such language, which occurs in all four Gospels and in the Acts of the Apostles is only intelligible when used to refer to a corporeal object, and there can be no doubt that its usage implies belief in a literal, physical resuscitation of Jesus' corpse.

However there are some features in the Gospel accounts which suggest a somewhat different meaning; there is talk of Jesus being able to pass through locked doors and of appearing and disappearing at will.[32] There also is mention of some difficulty in recognising him,[33] and according to St Matthew when Jesus was seen by his disciples for the last time 'they worshipped him but some doubted'.[34] We are not told what they doubted, but presumably they doubted that there was actually anything there to be seen. Such language implies that the resurrection of Jesus was not quite so straightforwardly physical as some of the other elements in the Gospel stories suggest.

When we turn to the letters of St Paul we find a non-literal usage of resurrection language. For Paul affirms resurrection while denying that 'flesh and blood' can ever experience it,[35] and while declaring that our stomachs will permanently perish.[36] Yet there can be no doubt at all that St Paul understood himself to be affirming a resurrection belief, for he declares it to be the *sine qua non* for Christian faith: 'if Christ was not raised, then our Gospel is null and void, and so is your faith'.[37]

On Paul's usage of resurrection language, to ask the question of how dead bodies can be raised is 'senseless'.[38] For him resurrection necessarily implies rising to a wholly new kind of life. Consider the sustained contrast he makes between the two modes of existence: earthly is contrasted with heavenly, perishable with imperishable, humiliation with glory, weakness with power, and animal with spiritual.[39] Such contrasts would be wholly beside the point if St Paul were thinking in terms of a physical rising.

In Philippians 1.22–4 Paul declares himself 'torn two ways' between his desire to 'depart' (from this life) in order to 'be with Christ', and his wish to 'stay on in the body' for the sake of his fellow Christians. He expresses a similar sentiment in 2 Corinthians 5.8 where he says he would like to leave his home in the body to go to live with the Lord. Neither of these statements makes any kind of sense unless we suppose that Paul took for granted that Jesus also had permanently left his home in the body.

This suggests that the Easter message as St Paul had received it did not include the empty tomb tradition, or the stories of Jesus eating and drinking with his disciples. Certainly Paul makes no allusion to such accounts, but places the whole weight of his appeal on the resurrection appearances of Jesus to his disciples. Moreover while the Gospel accounts talk of Jesus being 'seen' by his apostles, St Paul uses the deponent form 'ophthe' which according to Professor C. F. Evans 'cannot be translated "he was seen by" but means "he let himself be seen"'.[40] It is normally used to refer to spiritual vision, rather than physical sighting. Such a use of 'ophthe' is consistent with Paul's view that the appearances of Jesus to his disciples were similar in kind to the experience he himself had enjoyed on the road to Damascus.[41] That was quite explicitly an inward vision; 'God revealed his Son within me' is a literal translation of Galatians 1.15, and in Acts 26.19 Paul calls his experience 'a heavenly vision'. He had no doubt of its reality. This vision transformed his whole life. Yet Paul was quite sure that it was no resuscitated body that he saw, but rather a vision of the glory that lies ahead. For while it was a physical body that was buried, it was a spiritual body that was raised.[42] The same position is also expounded by the author of the first letter of Peter in which we read 'in the body (Jesus) was put to death; in the spirit he was brought to life'.[43]

We are therefore presented with two radically different usages of resurrection discourse. The language of the four Gospels and of the

Acts of the Apostles implies that Jesus' dead body was physically raised from the tomb, and was apprehended by the physical sense organs of the disciples. The language of Paul and I Peter suggests that 'Jesus' left his home in the body at death, and was raised to a new spiritual existence. He subsequently appeared to the minds of his disciples through 'a heavenly vision' and convinced them of his victory over death. I do not myself believe that these two pictures can be reconciled, and since the accounts of Paul and I Peter present an internally coherent picture their testimony seems more compelling. For there are a number of features in the empty tomb story which are decidedly odd. One is of course the difficulty of reconciling the stress on the physical character of Jesus' risen body, with the accounts of it passing through locked doors and appearing and disappearing at will. Another is the presence of angels as chief actors in the drama, which casts further doubt on its historical reliability.[44] The doubt is increased by the contradiction between the repeated assertion in Luke and Acts that throughout the time of Jesus' appearances the disciples did not leave the environs of Jerusalem, while both John and Matthew give accounts of resurrection appearances in Galilee.[45] Moreover the disagreement over precisely which women were the original witnesses to the supposed empty tomb adds further confusion to the story.[46]

But by far the most telling objection to the empty tomb tradition is the fact that St Mark's Gospel in its original form ends with an account of three women finding the tomb of Jesus empty and the report that they 'said nothing to anyone about it for they were afraid'. Here is yet another radical inconsistency for the accounts in Matthew, Luke, John and the second century appendix to St Mark speak of the women rushing off to tell the disciples, and of the disciples outrunning one another in their eagerness to see the tomb.[47] But much more significant than the discrepancy between the Gospels is that Mark, who is certainly the earliest and usually held to be the most reliable historically, should make this comment at all. For it implies that the empty tomb story formed no part of the generally received oral traditions about Jesus which circulated before the Gospels were written. It would be manifestly absurd for Mark to write that the women said nothing about it to anyone, if the story of their finding the empty tomb were generally known. The comment in fact only makes sense if Mark was conscious that he was adding a new element to the generally received traditions about Jesus; an element which was not known prior to the publication of his Gospel, and which he therefore had to account for by claiming that his sources had hitherto kept this knowledge secret out of fear.

That the story of the empty tomb was unknown before the appearance of Mark's Gospel, would tie in with the absence, which we have already noted, of any reference to it in the letters of St Paul. And the silence of 1 Peter is significant whether or not it was actually written by the Apostle in whose name it stands. If the letter came from Peter, his stress on the non-physical character of Jesus' rising is very powerful evidence against the empty tomb. But equally if the letter comes from an anonymous admirer of Peter writing in the time of Trajan his silence on the empty tomb would show how very late that tradition was to establish itself in the Church.

Mark's explanation for the empty tomb story not being known before his Gospel, namely that the women said nothing about it to anyone, is frankly incredible. Are we seriously to suppose that Mary the Mother of James would have withheld so telling a piece of supporting evidence from her son for over thirty years, and then have told Mark all about it? And are we to attribute silence through fear to those courageous women who, when all Jesus' male disciples forsook him and fled, followed him to Calvary?[48]

It would seem far more likely that the reason for the absence of the empty tomb tradition during the first three decades of the Church's life was that it lacked an historical foundation, and played no part in the original resurrection faith.[49] It would however be wholly natural for such an interpretation of the resurrection to develop later. We know that the first disciples were totally convinced of the reality and 'objectivity' of the visions they had seen. Without such conviction, the birth of the Christian Church is unintelligible. Yet the very strength of their certainty concerning the reality of the visions might lead their hearers to interpret their accounts in an increasingly physical character. And this development would be enhanced by their belief that Jesus' life, death and resurrection were all 'in accordance with the scriptures',[50] i.e. foretold in Messianic prophecies from the Old Testament. In the case of the resurrection, the scriptural text cited in two of the sermons reported in the Acts of the Apostles is Psalm 16.10. In the Septuagint translation this says, 'Thou wilt not let thy holy one see corruption'.[51] How easy it would be for a sermon from this text which sought to emphasise as strongly as possible the reality of the Easter visions, to be understood as teaching the literal rising again of Jesus' body!

However the ultimate triumph of a physicalist understanding of Jesus' resurrection has exercised a baneful influence on the Christian hope, for it transformed the spiritual understanding of resurrection into the ruthlessly physical doctrine of the resurrection of this flesh, which became dominant in Christian thought from the second century until comparatively recent times. For the reasons I set out in the previous chapter, this hope has now faded from the Christian consciousness, yet the literal understanding of Jesus' resurrection remains widespread. This leads to a radical incoherence in much contemporary Christian teaching. For a physical resurrection of Jesus is often preached on Easter Day, as grounds for belief in a non-physical resurrection of ourselves after death. The non-sequential character of such an argument seems to be insufficiently realised by the preacher, but the fact that the conclusion does not follow from the premise may help to explain the relative ineffectuality of the argument. For people often intuitively sense that an argument does not ring true even when they may not be able to articulate where it goes wrong. It would therefore seem wise for Christians to reconsider the teaching of St Paul about the nature and meaning of the resurrection hope both in relation to Jesus and to their own future destiny.

I have already mentioned that on two occasions Paul talks of departing from his present body. We should note however that his use of such terminology in no sense implies an expectation that he would henceforth live in a disembodied state. For he goes on to insist that in this new condition, 'we shall not find ourselves naked', but rather our 'inner nature' will have 'a new body put on over it so that out mortal part may be absorbed into life immortal'.[52]

It must be acknowledged that Paul is not entirely consistent, since at times he talks of our present bodies being changed or transfigured while at other times he talks of them being 'demolished'.[53] Professor G. W. H. Lampe suggests that St Paul is 'evidently groping after the idea that "we", that is our personalities, will be remade by God for a different mode of existence from that of the flesh-and-blood body, and yet that at the same time we shall retain our identity and be the same personalities as those which now live in the mode of physical beings'. In St Paul's thought the new 'spiritual bodies' will be a 'mode of self-identification and self-expression corresponding, in a spiritual existence, to the physical body in our earthly existence'.[54]

But how meaningful is this usage of resurrection language?

Clearly it represents a movement away from the primary and
original use of the term. Strictly speaking only that which falls can
'rise again'. St Paul defends his shift of meaning by pointing out
that we sow naked grain in the ground, but God clothes the grain
with a new body of his choice, and a wheat stalk comes up. So what
rises need not be precisely identical with what falls into the
ground.[55] This analogy cannot be pressed very far, for there is
absolute physical continuity between grain and wheat, but perhaps
we may take Paul's basic point that continuity is compatible with
change, as long as the basic principle of what we are continues.

If my argument in the previous chapter for identifying our self-
hood with the subject of our conscious experiences is valid, then I
suggest Paul's use of resurrection language is meaningful. It is a
'resurrection' hope because it declares that 'we ourselves' will
receive new bodies for the continued growth and development of
our personalities in heaven. But language has to be shared. How far
is Paul's usage generally intelligible? It seems from inter-testa-
mental Jewish writings that the meaning of the word 'resurrection'
had been extended at an early date to cover doctrines which in no
way implied the future resuscitation of the corpse.[56] And among St
Paul's contemporaries we may note that according to G. R. Driver,
the Covenanters of Qumran 'had some vague notion of physical
resurrection, and certainly believed in a future angelic existence with
God . . . but perhaps not in any resurrection of the body'.[57] Jesus
himself seems to have shared a comparable position. We know that
he regarded the pharisees' literal understanding of resurrection as
'quite wrong', and yet he believed in a resurrection hope provided it
was clearly understood that it in no sense entailed a continuation of
the conditions and relationships of earthly existence: 'when the dead
rise to life, they will be like the angels in heaven and will not marry',
is his one recorded comment on the resurrection state.[58]

When we turn from the New Testament to modern Christian
usage, we find that a position very like that of St Paul is fairly
common. According to the Archbishop's Commission on *Doctrine in
the Church of England*, 'in the life of the world to come the soul or spirit
will still have its appropriate organ of expression and activity'.[59] A
survey of modern Christian writing on the future hope shows that
this remains the most commonly accepted understanding of
resurrection today, even though most contemporary writers prefer
to use some circumlocution like 'the essential part of what we are'
rather than the somewhat unfashionable term 'soul'.[60] But what-

ever the preferred terminology, the sense is that the 'self' lives on and receives a new body for the continued expression of its thought and feeling. I suggest that this understanding of 'resurrection' passes the 'meaning is use' test, since we can show that such a meaning for the word 'resurrection' is presupposed by St Paul, and has been taken over by a number of modern writers. Consequently although it is not the literal meaning of the word 'resurrection', it is nevertheless no idiosyncratic usage of the term, but one that enjoys a wide currency.

I suggest that it can therefore be regarded as an intelligible possibility provided we are satisfied on two counts: first that our self-hood can be legitimately identified with our 'inner life', and secondly that it is possible that a resurrection world could exist in which re-embodiment could be supposed to take place. (This second condition is one which I have discussed at length elsewhere,[61] and to which I shall return briefly in the final chapter.) Provided these two conditions can be met then 'resurrection of the body' would seem a meaningful possibility.

This understanding of the doctrine of the resurrection in part depends on the continuity of our self-hood through bodily death. As such it is related to the other ancient Christian belief, the doctrine of the immortality of the soul. These two doctrines are not of course identical in meaning since some might suppose that a soul might permanently continue in a disembodied state. However, historically speaking the two doctrines have in the western tradition gone hand in hand, with the soul's immortality being seen as the link which provides for personal continuity between the two embodiments.

But the soul is a notoriously elusive concept. Long ago Justin Martyr lamented that 'philosophers cannot tell what a soul is',[62] and St Jerome described the concept as 'one of the greatest problems with which the Church has to deal'.[63] A contemporary writer could easily make the same comment for the issues remain as hard to define and as problematic as ever. Professor D. Z. Phillips has, however, made a potentially significant claim, namely that if we attend to the actual usuage of soul language we will realise that, correctly understood, it has no reference to any supposed future life. Consequently he holds that belief in survival of death is not a necessary condition of belief in immortality. This sounds paradoxical, but Phillips holds that this is because we do not normally examine our language with sufficient care.

According to Phillips, language relating to the soul, to

immortality, or eternity refers not to a life beyond but to what we value here and now. 'Questions about the state of a man's soul are questions about the kind of life he is living'.[64] Talk of a man's soul refers 'to the complex set of practices and beliefs which acting with integrity would cover for that person . . . it is a kind of talk bound up with certain moral or religious reflections a man may make . . . . Once this is recognised, once one ceases to think of the soul . . . as some kind of incorporeal substance, one can be brought to see that in certain contexts talk about the soul is . . . to be understood in terms of the kind of life a person is living'.[65] Likewise Phillips believes that 'eternal life is the reality of goodness', and that 'the immortality of the soul refers to the state an individual is in relation to the unchanging reality of God'.[66] Not surprisingly therefore Phillips believes that 'speculations about continued existence after death are beside the point'.[67]

There is no doubt that Phillips is right in saying that 'in certain contexts' this is what is meant by talk of the soul. In fact a consultation with the Concise Oxford English Dictionary would show that Phillips' examples cover six of the ten meanings there recorded, even if they do leave out what that Dictionary considers to be the word's primary sense. But what conclusions follow from the fact that when a word has several meanings, one can compose sentences which illustrate some of these meanings but not others? Consider how easy it would be to invent sentences which illustrate the meaning of the word 'element' as when one talks of a man being in his element, or being exposed to the elements, or possessing knowledge of the elements of a particular subject, or covering the element of his kettle with water. Yet none of these examples gives the slightest hint of the meaning the word has when used in chemistry. Likewise consider the word 'heart'; one could give pages of examples of its use to describe the inmost emotions and feelings, yet none of this would invalidate the fact that for a surgeon the heart is a physical organ which pumps blood around the human body.

So too with the word 'soul'. Of course much talk of the soul relates to moral or religious evaluations of the person's state in the here and now. If we say that a person has 'sold his soul to a particular cause' we are reflecting critically on a fanatical devotion of which we do not approve; and if we refer to a jazz musician as 'playing with soul' we mean that he has conveyed a sense of deep if sentimental emotion through his music. But neither of these is an appropriate context in which to ascertain the meaning of the word 'soul' in relation to the question of immortality. To discover that we should turn to its usage in the context of death and dying.

Let us consider therefore the way the word 'soul' is used in 'The Pastoral Case of the Dying' and in the Prayer Book Funeral Service. For the former I shall take examples from the book of that title,[68] and from *The Priests' Book of Private Devotions*,[69] both of which are in common usage today. In one Litany for the Dying we read, 'In the last moments of this painful life below; in the awful parting of soul and body; in the hour of death; and in the day of judgement; Defend and deliver his soul, O Lord'. In the Litany for the Dead the response is 'Give rest to the souls of the faithful departed'.[70] In the prayers prescribed for use at the bedside of the dying we come across the following: 'Go forth, O Christian Soul, from this world . . . . As thy soul departeth from the body, may the bright hosts of angels receive thee . . . Receive, O Lord, the soul of thy servant . . . Save his soul at the hour of its departure from the body, open to him the gate of life'.[71] The rubrics endorse this picture by prescribing what the priest should repeat 'to help the departing soul' or what he should say 'if the soul lingers', and what should be said 'when the soul has departed'.[72] The Prayer Book Funeral Service takes up such language: 'Forasmuch as it hath pleased Almighty God of his great mercy to take unto himself the soul of our dear brother here departed: we therefore commit his body to the ground'.

One has only to read such prayers or parallels to them in the Roman Missal or in the prayers prescribed by the Russian Orthodox Church for use 'at the departing of the soul'[73] to realise the inadequacy of Phillips' analysis of soul-talk in the actual context of death and dying. In such a context it is nonsense to say that talk of the soul should be understood in terms of the kind of life a man is leading, and I suggest that it is this context which matters if one is really considering what the religious hope of immortality means. These prayers express the view that the soul is an incorporeal substance which departs from the body at death, and which also constitutes the real person. For although the prayers seem at times to suggest that the soul is a 'thing' which departs, they also make it clear that the departing soul can be rightly regarded as the person himself: 'May the angels receive *thee*, open to *him* the gate of life'. This is perhaps brought out most clearly in the Anglican Funeral Service when the priest says 'Almighty God, with whom do live the spirits of them that depart hence in the Lord, and with whom the souls of the faithful, after they are delivered from the burden of the

flesh, are in joy and felicity; we give thee hearty thanks, for that it
hath pleased thee to deliver this our brother out of the miseries of
this sinful world'. Here the 'spirit' or 'soul' is seen as something
belonging to the man, some part of man which has 'departed
hence', and yet, at the same time is something which *is* the man,
something which can be identified with 'this our brother'. Now
whether such an identification is possible is precisely the problem
we discussed in the previous chapter. But the issue cannot be side-
stepped by D. Z. Phillips' attempt to give an entirely this-world
sense to talk of the soul. Any such attempt must fail if we take with
any seriousness the criterion Phillips elsewhere adopts of 'meaning is
use', and consider the actual usage in the relevant context.

A similar argument applies against those who, like Nicholas
Lash, talk of 'eternal life' as if this were to be contrasted with talk of
'life after death'. Lash asserts that 'eternal life is *this* life, experienced
not in successiveness but in simultaneity'.[74] Karl Barth declares that
'eternal life is not another, second life beyond our present one, but
the reverse side of *this* life, as God sees it'.[75] And Paul Tillich writes,
'Participation in eternity is not life hereafter . . . eternal life does
not mean a continuation of temporal life after death'.[76] To all such
assertions it is possible to show that from the point of view of both the
New Testament and the Christian tradition, they are proposing a
novel linguistic usage in saying that eternal life refers *exclusively* to
the present. John's Gospel certainly teaches that eternal life can be
experienced now: 'This is eternal life: to know thee who alone art
God, and Jesus Christ whom thou hast sent'.[77] And on eleven other
occasions in this Gospel and five times in the first letter of John we
find a similar message presented.[78] Yet the conviction that it is
possible here and now to enter into an eternal relationship with God
so far from precluding a life after death, presupposes it. For the
strongest religious argument for life after death has always been that
if man in this life can truly enter a relationship with God which God
values, then the eternal Creator will not allow that relationship to
be destroyed by death. Certainly St John explicitly teaches that
eternal life will endure through bodily death[79] and that it is what
God promised us for the future[80] as well as something we may
partially experience in the present.

St Paul adopts a similar approach. 'The free gift of God is eternal
life',[81] a present reality, and yet it is always linked in Paul's mind
with the hope of immortality, and an 'eternal weight of glory
beyond all comparison with this earthly life'.[82] In the Synoptic

Gospels eternal life is always something we are to inherit in the age to come[83] and this exclusively future reference is also seen in the Pastoral Epistles, the letter to the Hebrews, and the two letters of Peter.[84]

If we turn to the Christian tradition there can be no doubt that eternal life has always been understood to have a future reference, sometimes even to the extent of undervaluing the present reality of man's contact with the eternal. This could be abundantly demonstrated from the prayers and hymns of all Christian traditions and the writings of its theologians throughout the centuries,[85] but it is hardly necessary to labour this point since no one could really suppose that the funeral prayer 'Requiem Aeternam' refers to this life only!

On the other hand it could be argued that the Christian tradition has not taken sufficiently seriously the fact that it has predominantly expressed its prayers for the departed in terms of 'eternal rest'. For to rest for ever seems hardly consistent with talk of a fully personal life being continued. On the other hand the phrase 'eternal rest', taken in isolation, might be thought to accord well with the increasingly popular modern view that after death we will cease to exist as conscious personal beings, but will live for ever in the consciousness of God. I have often been puzzled by the fact that no exponent of this view has (to the best of my knowledge) appealed to the concept of eternal rest in support of this theory. This may be because the prayer has never been regarded as expressing a doctrinal position, or perhaps because those who champion the idea of our life being remembered are anxious to present their view as a way of articulating Christian belief in a future life. So let us examine the arguments they have adduced and see how far the theory might be thought to give expression to the Christian hope.

Charles Hartshorne is the best known exponent of the view that we will 'live on in the complete and infallible memory of God'.[86] According to Hartshorne, 'He to whom all hearts are open remains evermore open to any heart that ever was apparent to him. What we once were to him, less than that we can never be, for otherwise he himself as knowing us would lose something of his own reality . . . Hence if we can never be less than we have been to God, we can in reality never be less than we have been . . . Death cannot be the destruction, or even the fading of the book of one's life; it can only mean the fixing of its concluding page. Death writes "The End" upon the last page, but nothing further happens to the book, by way of either addition or subtraction'.[87] As John Hick rightly points out Hartshorne's reasoning is profoundly ambiguous. Strictly speaking his argument only says that God's present awareness of us will not fade, but his statement 'we can in reality never be less than we have been' gives the seriously misleading impression 'that the state of being remembered . . . constitutes as full and real existence as the state of being alive. But this is manifestly false'.[88]

There is all the difference in the world between actually living, and simply being remembered, even if that memory consisted of all one's thoughts, words and deeds recorded in a divine 'book of life' in the way both Hartshorne and Pittenger suggest.[89] Consider for example the medieval notion of a day of judgement 'when the secrets of all hearts shall be disclosed'. Thomas of Celano pictures the reading of the supposed 'book of life' thus:

'Lo the book exactly worded,
Wherein all hath been recorded:
Doom shall pass with deed accorded.

Then the Judge will sit, revealing
Every hidden thought and feeling,
Unto each requital dealing.

What shall I, frail man be pleading,
Who for me be interceding,
When the just are mercy needing?'[90]

This whole picture only makes sense if the trembling sinner standing before the divine judgement seat is different from the complete and infallible knowledge of the sinner's past which is possessed by the Judge. And the idea of hell is so terrible because it is assumed that it would involve living persons being thrown into the lake of fire. If it were only a question of the record of a person's life being consigned to the flames, or the memory of a person's existing being blotted out, our personal fear would be nothing like as great.

It might be objected at this point that since neither I, nor the writers I am discussing,[91] believe in a Last Judgement, it is irrelevant to ask whether or not their picture of a future life is compatible with it. But I use this imagery only to illustrate the radical difference between an existing person, and the full and infallible knowledge about that person which God possesses. And if we reject the notion of hell, and believe with Madame de Staël that 'to know all is to forgive all',[92] the difference remains just as apparent.

However, I may be underestimating what could be entailed in the concept of God remembering us. According to David Edwards, 'God's memory of us will be more powerful and altogether better than our ówn memories', and because God remembers us we will 'share in God's life and God's glory, when nothing is between God and us'.[93] Edwards quotes St Augustine's saying, 'after this life God himself will be our place', and he draws attention to the opening verses of II Peter in which it is argued that because divine power enables 'us to know the One who called us by his own splendour and might . . . (we will) come to share in the very being of God'.[94] This idea of sharing in the very being of God is taken up by the Spanish philosopher Unamuno who argues that to be remembered by God is 'to have my consciousness sustained by the Supreme consciousness',[95] or as Peter Hamilton puts it, 'everything of any value in our life will be . . . immortalized in (God's) supremely personal life'.[96]

The point these writers are making is that God's memory of us would not be limited to a memory of our external behaviour in the way that our memories of other people necessarily are. For God knows us from within. He not only knows me, he also knows what it is like to be me; what it is like to think, feel, will and decide as Paul Badham. If God is literally omniscient this conclusion necessarily follows. And this is spelt out beautifully in Psalm 139.

> 'Lord you have examined me and you know me . . .
> You understand all my thoughts . . .
> You know all my actions,
> Even before I speak,
> You already know what I will say . . .
> Your knowledge of me is too deep;
> It is beyond my understanding.'[97]

Moreover since God is outside time, this knowledge of me will remain permanently in God's present awareness. When I am dead it will not strictly be a question of God remembering me, as if he had to recall to mind past knowledge, for to God no knowledge is past. And hence my life will exist for ever in the eternal consciousness of God.

But there are serious problems with this position. For although God may indeed understand all my thoughts and know why I think and feel as I do he cannot think my thoughts for me, not simply because an all-good and all-wise deity cannot think thoughts which may sometimes be evil and are often mistaken, but also because thoughts can only be 'owned' by a single subject of consciousness. Of course there is a sense in which more than one person can have 'the same thought', just as they could each separately write down that thought in 'identical sentences'. But the sentences could never be numerically identical, although each would be, to use C. S. Peirce's terminology 'a token of the same type'.[98] Likewise for the thoughts, no matter how 'identical' they might be in the one sense of that word, they would each remain uniquely distinct, in that each would have been thought by a different individual.

Consequently when I die the subject of my conscious experiences cannot be absorbed into the divine mind; and although an omniscient God cannot forget me, and indeed a timeless God must experience me as ever-present, the fact remains that if there is no personal life after death then, even though God 'remembers' me, I will be no more. I appreciate that many may find comfort in Pittenger's argument that 'with God, and in God, everything is for ever safe–and safe in the one way in which it can be enduringly secure, namely in God's valuing and receiving it into the divine life to be treasured there for ever'.[99] Yet I simply do not feel that this argument rings true. In what sense can even God be said to 'value' and 'treasure' everything? Other thinkers in this tradition have spelt out how literally this claim must be taken. Karl Rahner speaks of 'the history of the world as a whole' entering eternal life;[100] John Macquarrie explicitly mentions 'long extinct animals'[101] and Berdyaev insists that 'every blade of grass' is to be included.[102] At this point I feel the argument collapses under the weight of its own rhetoric. It is so all-embracing as to be without any real meaning.

But even if we confine the argument to human existence, is it really possible to affirm that every actual human life has been lived in such a way as to 'enrich' the being of God? Pittenger says that he is able to assert the 'abiding worth of our mortal span of years, such that our having existed at all can be said to have dignity and value'.[103] But can this be validly said of all the countless millions whose lives have been blighted by slavery, war, famine, ignorance and sin? It is one thing to affirm that every human personality is of potential value such that God in a future life might be able to bring good out of them, but it is quite another to affirm that every actual lived existence will be treasured in God's memory.

Moreover this doctrine faces one very substantial obstacle in the way of its establishing itself as a 'Christian' belief and that is that there is no support whatever for it in the New Testament, or in nineteen hundred years of Christian tradition. It should therefore be seen as a substitute for, rather than an expression of, the Christian hope.[104] Pittenger rightly says that the idea corresponds to some Old Testament usage for in the absence of any fuller hope during most of the Old Testament period, all that could be hoped for was that one might be remembered, and one's name not be 'blotted out'.[105] But there is no hint of any taking up of this Old Testament usage within the New, despite the fact that David Edwards quotes two texts in alleged support of his position. The first of these which we cited earlier when expounding Edwards' position, comes from 2 Peter 1.4 and talks of us coming 'to share in the very being of God'. However, this in no sense implies a view that we are to be incorporated into the divine memory. For the context makes it clear that this very Greek-orientated author understood our partaking of the divine nature in the sense of our gaining freedom from being dominated by our passions and hence to some extent sharing in the impassibility of God. 2 Peter certainly believed in a life after death. He supposed he would shortly be leaving his lodging in this present body, and would gain admission into the eternal Kingdom of Jesus Christ. And his ultimate hope was for life on 'a new earth' which he supposed would follow the destruction of the present universe.[106] In short his understanding of eternal life was that it would involve the immortality of the soul to be followed at a later stage by a new life in a resurrection world.

Edwards' second text comes from Luke 23.43, and is the petition of the thief crucified alongside Jesus. According to Edwards the thief realised 'what kind of destiny is revealed on the cross of Jesus' and therefore said 'Jesus, remember me when you come to your throne'.[107] But are we seriously to suppose that what the thief wanted was for his previous criminal life to be preserved for ever in Christ's memory? I suggest that if the petition were seriously meant, the man was seeking to safeguard his future, rather than to immortalise his past. Hence his request to be remembered should be interpreted as a wish to be allowed to enter into the heavenly Kingdom to which he believed Jesus was passing. Certainly Jesus' reply would back up such an interpretation: 'Today you will be with me in Paradise'. And if authority is to be seen anywhere in the story it must lie in Jesus' response, rather than in a profoundly unlikely meaning read into the thief's request.

The idea of living for ever in God's memory might seem attractive to modern historians of Christian thought like Edwards, Pittenger or Macquarrie through whose own writings many luminaries of the past have lived again. But I suggest that the notion would have had no appeal to the intensely future-orientated Church of the first century. For them the hope of heaven entailed the 'passing away of the old order', and of God 'making all things new'.[108] And in fact it is an amusing exercise to take a concordance and look up the New Testament contexts of words like 'hope', 'inherit' or 'heirs' and see just how impossible it would be to interpret such texts as a wish for their present life to be preserved in God's memory. The future St Paul looks forward to with such enthusiasm could never be interpreted as an expectation that God would remember Paul's past life. And the spread of the Christian Gospel throughout the world would have been unthinkable if the Christian hope had originally been proclaimed and understood as permanent life in God's memory.

I conclude therefore that the language of resurrection and immortality has no clear meaning or agreed usage outside the context of belief in life after death, and that language of eternal life although referring in part to present experience nevertheless, in the usage of the New Testament and the Christian tradition, always conveys a further connotation of a future destiny. I also conclude that the meaning of life after death cannot be adequately expressed in terms of God 'remembering' us.

On the other hand I hope I have shown that at least one form of the doctrine of resurrection is intelligible, and that the notion that the soul or consciousness could survive death is at least sufficiently intelligible to explore further. Neither of these doctrines may be true, in the sense of corresponding to reality. The discussion in these first two chapters has simply been clearing the ground, so that the arguments for and against these notions may now proceed.

Part Two

3 The Naturalistic Case for Extinction

The strongest argument against our immortality is the fact that each of us 'owns' a body with a datable origin, and our conscious personal self comes into being, grows and develops in the closest possible relationship to that body.[1] Hence on all reasonable analogy our selfhood could be expected to perish when our bodies die. This argument was expressed with characteristic lucidity in David Hume's classic essay 'On the Immortality of the Soul':

> 'Where any two objects are so closely connected that all alterations which we have ever seen in the one are attended with proportional alterations in the other; we ought to conclude by all rules of analogy, that, when there are still greater alterations produced in the former, and it is totally dissolved, there follows a total dissolution of the latter . . . The weakness of the body and that of the mind in infancy are exactly proportioned; their vigour in manhood, their sympathetic disorder in sickness, their common gradual decay in old age. The step further seems unavoidable; their common dissolution in death'.[2]

This argument was not original to Hume. Many centuries earlier it had been employed by the early Christian writer Arnobius in his argument for the necessity of literal bodily resurrection. He asks 'Can any one say . . . why the soul which is said . . . to be immortal . . . is sick in men who are sick, senseless in children, and worn out in doting, silly, and crazy old age?'[3] And this same point has been made in our own day by Lady Oppenheimer who asserts: 'Human beings are thoroughly mortal. It is odd that we should expect the soul to outlast the body, when as far as we can see it perishes first'.[4]

This argument can easily be formulated and understood on the basis of our common experience of life. We need no special study of human physiology or psychology to know that our thinking is strongly influenced by our bodily condition. We need only have a cold, a toothache, or consume some alcohol to be aware that what happens to the body affects the mind. Nevertheless this argument is powerfully supported by the way in which the sciences of genetics, endocrinology and neurophysiology can help to pinpoint precisely how it is that our mental health depends on our physical endowment, and on the correct functioning of our various bodily parts.

Professor John Hick sums up the findings of modern geneticists by saying that, 'our temperamental type and character structure, our intelligence, our imaginative range and special aptitudes, all develop in directions and within limits that are genetically prescribed'.[5] To this genetic endowment we must add the specific contribution of our endocrine system which is partly determined by our genes, and partly by the nutritional quality of our diet and water supply, and the condition of the particular organs. For instance if our drinking water contains less than half a microgramme of iodine per litre our thyroid gland will not function properly, and in consequence we will find mental activity difficult, memory and powers of concentration will weaken, and we will lack initiative and drive in our lives.[6] And if our parathyroids fail to keep the level of calcium in our blood supply above eight milligrams per hundred millilitres we will be irritable and disagreeable.[7] Likewise if our adrenals cause too much salt to be excreted, or if we fail to consume sufficient salt then we will suffer from intellectual lassitude, incapacity for mental arithmetic and lack of judgement.[8] Similarly if we eat too little or too infrequently to keep up our blood-sugar level we will become emotionally unstable, irritable and inefficient, and the same consequences would follow from any disorder in the Islets of Langerhans in the pancreas which control the level of sugar in our blood.[9] In fact as Dr A. E. Clark-Kennedy affirms, our endocrine system sets 'the level at which all our instincts and feelings are geared'.[10] And Professor V. H. Mottram argues that the correct functioning of these organs is so important to our individuality that they can be called 'the glands of personality'.[11]

In the field of neurophysiology there is virtually unanimous agreement that all our thinking, feeling and willing is directly related to particular brain states. Conflict arises only about the nature of this relationship. For the old-fashioned materialist, mind is simply an epiphenomenon of the brain, a product of brain states and of no causative significance or explanatory value. A more sophisticated materialism challenges this view, and argues that the language of mind which we use to refer to our own inner experiences, can never be equated with, or reduced to language of brain processes. Nevertheless its exponents believe that both language systems ultimately refer to a single referent, the complex but irreducibly physical organism with which we think and feel. And the only rival to this position to enjoy any kind of support at present is a neo-Cartesian dualism according to which mind and brain are distinct entities which nonetheless interact at all times during our present embodied existence, so that changes in brain states will always affect our minds, and mental change will correspondingly affect our brains.

Since both modern materialists and neo-Cartesians agree about the factual concomitance of mental and physical change it is hard to see how any experimental data could definitively establish either position at least with regard to all the normal facts of human experiencing even though the balance might shift in favour of Cartesianism if the data of psychical research were to be generally regarded as evidential.[12] However for our present purposes the significant point is the agreement of both parties that our mental life is intimately bound up with the growth and development of our bodies in general and of our brains in particular. And this must call in question the likelihood of our surviving bodily death. This is obvious in the case of a materialist theory for there could be no sense in continuing to use the language of mind after the mechanism on which mental life depends has been dissolved. But it is also an issue for the Cartesian theory. For having postulated that mind and brain interact at every point from conception to the day of our dying so that there is always a direct causal relationship between the two entities it is odd to stop at death's door, and to say that at this point their interaction ceases and the mind continues in being while the body dies. Clearly it is not logically impossible to postulate this, but the oddness of doing so needs to be stressed.

Moreover there are particular problems in talking of the human 'mind' surviving bodily death when we cannot intelligibly say when this 'mind' comes into existence. It is vital for talk of personal survival of bodily death that what survives should be what I really am, and we defined this in chapter 1 by saying that 'I am the subject of my conscious experiences'. Yet it seems impossible for anyone to name a particular time when this 'subject' comes into being.

Clearly there is a sense in which my distinctive life goes back to the moment of conception, for at that point my unique DNA code came into existence, bearing the genetic inheritance which to so great an extent shaped what I am now. Yet 70 per cent of zygotes develop no further than this initial stage, and are expelled from the mother's body as foetal wastage in what she may experience simply as a late menstrual period.[13] It seems wholly unintelligible to suppose that 70 per cent of the future population of 'heaven' should be unformed zygotes, and modern developments only accentuate this problem. The intra-uterine device, usually known either by its initials or as 'the coil' works by preventing the implantation of fertilized ova, and so presumably must greatly increase the already high proportion of zygotes rejected in the course of nature.[14] And there is the problem of 'failed' test-tube babies, because for every baby born as a result of 'in vitro' conception, hundreds of successively fertilized human eggs grown in culture have been tipped down the sluice after reaching the sixteen-cell stage.[15]

Implantation of the cell in the mother's womb might seem an alternative possibility to mark the beginning of individual life. But we then face the problem of identical twins whose separation does not take place until perhaps the fourth week after implantation. Estimates vary between 4 per cent and 70 per cent of identical twins whose separation was subsequent to implantation,[16] and we can hardly suppose that in these cases the 'soul' split in two, up to four weeks after beginning life! Moreover at present one in five human pregnancies are terminated during the third month of gestation, giving a total of some thirty million abortions a year.[17] Once more we have to ask how intelligible it is to think of these rejected foetuses enjoying everlasting life in heaven, without ever having experienced independent life on earth.

Perhaps therefore we need to look again at the traditional concept of the 'animation' of the foetus as occurring when the mother feels the child 'quicken' in her womb. Unfortunately, however, the timing of this depends more on the mother's subjective interpretation of what is going on in her womb rather than on any clearly identifiable development in the child, though 'quickening' does tend to be reported at approximately the same time as the child's neurological equipment is substantially completed,[18] so the concept of 'animation' at this point might not be wholly vacuous. However it does seem very hard to describe even a supposedly 'animated' foetus as possessing a conscious personal self for detailed studies which have been made of babies and their development agree that the new born baby possesses no self-awareness, and that the distinction between self and not-self is one that the infant only acquires towards the end of its first two years of life.[19] Dr R. S. Lee sums up the position of the new born baby thus:

'His self or personality is only rudimentary at birth. He is a bundle of raw materials of personality, of potentialities for development, which belong together in one body and in the nucleus of a person. Both have to grow. They are only at the starting point of their growth to maturity. Body and mind alike will develop through the experience of living. The raw materials of personality have to be drawn together into the final result of one integrated human being . . . What the child becomes is limited by his inherited capacities, his native endowment; it also depends on what his family is like as individuals in themselves and as a social unit in which the baby has to find his place as a member'.[20]

Dr Stephen Rose illustrates the way in which the child's intellectual and emotional growth matches the anatomical and biochemical development of the human brain, and shows that consciousness emerges as neuronal connections sprout and, synapses are made.[21] Consequently there is no sense in attributing to the infant qualities of self-awareness, conscious thought, or purposive action until his nervous system and bodily organs have sufficiently developed for such capacities to exist. As Dr Anthony Smith points out: 'No amount of teaching, coaxing or practice will cause a baby or child to perform some skilled act until the necessary mechanisms in the nervous system are mature'.[22]

In fact society has always recognised that moral responsibility, intellectual discernment, and even readiness for religion are qualities which a baby does not possess, but which he gradually acquires in the course of his growth towards full personhood. In Imperial Japan a child became a person at the age of seven. In Britain, eight years old is the earliest one can be held in any way responsible enough to be considered capable of committing a crime, and full legal responsibility is not reached till the age of fourteen in the case of the criminal law, and eighteen in the case of civil law. In the field of religion, the Roman Church will not admit to communion before the age of seven, and the Anglican Church not before 'years of discretion' have been reached which is normally interpreted as meaning at least twelve years of age. This is also the practice of the Jewish community. Fourteen, sixteen, eighteen and twenty-one have each found favour in a number of societies as years for achieving legal, moral and social adulthood as a fully mature person.[23]

To the best of my knowledge there is no society which regards children below the age of five as persons in the fullest sense of that word. This has profound implications for belief in life after death for historically the vast majority of mankind has died before the age of five, and even today in many poorer communities it is the exception rather than the rule for babies to survive into adulthood.[24] On a global scale one in five of all babies die before the age of one,[25] and in many countries of the Third World the chances of living to the age of five remain no more than fifty-fifty.[26]

Strictly speaking the numbers involved are irrelevant to the problem posed by infant mortality which is simply that it is impossible for the conscious personal self of any individual to survive bodily death if that person dies before his consciousness has in any real sense developed. Yet somehow the sheer proportion of infant mortality tends to make the concept of life after death seem bizarre. One could imagine God making special arrangements for awkward cases, but it is harder to think in such terms when these cases turn out to be in the majority.

Moreover the problem is not confined to infant mortality. We have also to face the issue of the imbecile whose mind never develops, or the person afflicted by disease, injury, drugs or operation which radically change his personality. An operation formerly used to 'help' patients suffering from acute stress, known as a leucotomy (or lobotomy) has been discovered to be responsible for profound personality changes in those on whom it was performed. According to Carl Sagan this operation can destroy any continuing sense of self-hood – the feeling that I am a particular individual with some control over my life and circumstances.[27] Other consequences of the operation can be changes in character, behaviour patterns, moral values, religious sense and aesthetic appreciation. Localised brain lesions can have similar, if less dramatic effects on human personality.[28] Moreover it is wrong to ignore the impact of less tangible but no less real psychological or social pressures, and particularly the trauma which tragic experience has on human consciousness. And age alone has its special problems – thirty-six per cent of us will suffer from mental disorders in the course of our physical decline in old age.[29] Who then is the 'I' which will survie death?

If 'personality damage' occurs shortly before the body's dissolution it might seem plausible to look on it as a temporary derangement, and think that a healthy mind would be restored in the next life. But it becomes increasingly hard to think in such terms the longer the time interval has been since some profound personality change took place. Moreover 'profound change' only highlights the fact that even in normal circumstances change is actually ever-present in the human character and personality. Not for nothing does Gordon Lowe entitle his book *The Growth of Personality from Infancy to Old Age*.[30] For life is a continuous development, and this fact raises very serious difficulties in the way of talk of a constant personal self surviving the traumas of life and death.

St Augustine sought to solve the problem both of infant mortality and of senility by claiming that in the next life all would rise from the dead aged about thirty.[31] He argued that those who died as infants possessed the potentiality of adulthood, and hence God would convert their potential adulthood to actual adulthood for the resurrection life. Likewise the decline which sets in after the age of thirty would be reversed by divine power. But Augustine's solution does not face up to the gravity of the situation. For our adult personality is the product not simply of the genetic potential with which our life commences, but of all that happens to us during our actual life. Our personality is shaped by nurture as well as by nature, and neither contribution can be ignored if we want to gain an adequate insight into human development and growth. Moreover while thirty might have seemed the summit of human fullness in an age when few survived to their forties, many who now reach their seventies, while acknowledging some diminution of their mental and physical powers, might yet reasonably believe that the wisdom of their maturity represented an improvement on the foolishness of youth or the impatience of young adulthood. And they would rightly feel affronted by a system which would discount four decades or more of potential growth in those who live out the full human span. Hence Augustine's solution is altogether too facile.

I conclude therefore that the evidence of infant mortality, lifelong imbecility and of personality change in later life raise very serious difficulties against any concept of life after death. David Hume writes, 'when it is asked, whether Agamemnon, Thersites, Hannibal, Varro, and every stupid clown that ever existed in Italy, Scythia, Bactria or Guinea, are now alive; can any man think that a scrutiny of nature will furnish arguments strong enough to answer so strange a question in the affirmative?'.[32] Hume's argument could be strengthened if we ask not only about the heroes of antiquity and those lesser mortals Hume writes off as 'stupid clowns', but also of that half of humanity which died in infancy, and of those millions who lived out the whole of their earthly existence in a state of mental confusion.

No doubt it can be argued, as Austin Farrer does so well, that God will love and save whatever is there to be saved and loved, and that God will make no arbitrary discriminations.[33] Yet presumably even God must draw the line somewhere in the course of human development. Neither a fertilised ovum which fails even to achieve implantation, nor a foetus which goes to the full term of pregnancy without acquiring the necessary brain tissues can seriously be considered a future citizen of heaven. Yet as Jonathan Glover points out, 'the transition from fertilized egg to adult . . . can better be represented by a steady upward curve than by a series of obviously discrete stages with abrupt transitions'.[34] And likewise with our neurological equipment; it is not a question of either normality or total anacephaly, but of every possible gradation between the two.

Moreover the problem which arises when we look at the gradual development toward personhood of man as an individual, can be exactly paralleled by the problem of deciding at what stage in evolution mankind can be thought of as emerging as a species. Likewise if we are prepared to think of the consciousness of an eighteen month child as a suitable bearer of immortality this raises the question of the claims to immortality of equally intelligent and self-conscious animals.

Current evolutionary theory supposes man to be descended from Ramapithecus, an ape-like creature who lived between fourteen million and three million years ago.[35] According to Richard Leakey this creature began to diversify somewhere between five and six million years ago 'probably because climatic or other environmental changes formed new habitats for exploitation'.[36] Consequently by four million years ago Ramapithius had evolved into four different strains: Australopithicus robustus, Australopithicus africanus, Homo habilis, and a late verson of the original stock (which probably continued in being for another million years). The two Australopithicene species survived for three million years and then became extinct. Homo habilis by contrast gradually evolved into Homo erectus over the next million and a half years, and then equally gradually evolved into Homo sapiens.[37]

The case for regarding Habilis as Homo is that he could walk upright as well as we do, and his hands were almost as dexterous as ours. He made and used stone tools and probably constructed dwellings. His larynx would have enabled him to speak, and the shape of his skull indicates that his brain included Broca's area, the area generally associated with the use of language. A Habilis skull dated at two and a half million years old showed a brain capacity of 800 cc.,[38], which is twice that of a modern chimpanzee, and well on the way towards the 1100–2200 range of modern man.

However in all these respects Habilis only differs in degree from his Australopithicene cousins, and it has been a matter of debate whether they too should be described as human. Certainly Australopithicus robustus (robust southern ape) has also been termed Zinjanthropus (East African man) or Paranthropus (almost man or alongside man).[39] I suspect that the attribution of humanity is denied to these species primarily because they became extinct, whereas Habilis lies in our direct ancestry and over four million years evolved into what we are now.

At what point in the evolutionary chain our ancestors are described as human is of less importance than the fact that the line has to be drawn somewhere if man is held to enjoy an eternal destiny which apes are denied, and this raises difficulties. Ramapithicus is clearly an ape, Homo sapiens is clearly a man. But as is the rule for biological changes the evolutionary development between the two can best be represented by a rising curve rather than definitive steps. Terms like 'Habilis', 'Erectus' and 'Sapiens' are simply convenient generalisations for stages of development which imperceptibly succeed one another over four million years. But if man alone is immortal we must say that one generation of hominids were so ape-like that at death they passed into oblivion, while the next generation was sufficiently man-like to be heirs of eternal life. What would the children think of this? Would they know that their parents were 'only animals', while they themselves were a new kind of being? Moreover how could a line be drawn between two generations so precisely, when every family of that generation would be at a slightly different stage. Suppose an older 'ape-like' hominid married one of the new generation 'man-like' hominids, would the husband be mortal and the wife immortal? The more one tries to picture how such a divide could be made the more inconceivable it appears.

Moreover on what grounds could so great a distinction be justified? It may seem natural for modern man surrounded by the artefacts of his industrial civilisation to distance himself from the animal kingdom, expecially as the nearest surviving species to us diverged from our evolutionary ladder some twenty-eight million years ago.[40] But for three of the four million years man has existed, he lived in the African savannah a mode of life fairly close to that of two other hominid species to which he was closely related. This raises in its most acute form the question of why man should be considered so special. However at a lesser level precisely the same question can be raised in comparing man with other animals who still exist today.

David Hume as usual puts the issue clearly before us: 'animals undoubtedly feel, think, love, hate, will and even reason, though in a more imperfect manner than men: are their souls also immaterial and immortal?'.[41] Unless one is prepared to deny Hume's premise, his question is very much to the point. So is Hume right? Almost all the most influential schools of thought in the west would repudiate his assumption. For the Aristotelian-Thomist tradition man is a 'rational animal' distinguished from all other creatures by his powers of reason, and as such the owner not only of a mortal animal soul, but also of an immortal rational soul. For the Platonic-Cartesian tradition 'brutes not only have a smaller degree of reason than men, but are wholly lacking in it',[42] whereas man's essential being is characterised by the fact that he thinks. And though Charles Darwin and his immediate followers like T. H. Huxley, stressed the oneness of man with the animal kingdom, their Neo-Darwinian successors have been more impressed by the way man has evolved above his animal past, and though denying that man has a soul, nevertheless insist on the uniqueness of his mind.

Thus Julian Huxley asserts, 'not merely has conceptual thought been evolved only in man: it could not have been evolved except in man. There is but one path of unlimited progress through the evolutionary maze'.[43] Theodosius Dobzhansky writes, 'To me, my mind is the most immediate and indubitable of all certainties . . . I infer that other people also have minds . . . For animals . . . the evidence is wholly unreliable'.[44] Dobzhansky claims that man alone is capable of reflection, of self-consciousness, and of an awareness that he will die. He also thinks that 'if the zoological classification were based on psychological instead of mainly morphological traits, man would have been considered a separate phylum or even kingdom'.[45]

The belief that man alone can think is deeply entrenched among many of the leading biologists of today, with man's use of language being taken as key behavioural evidence of this unique ability.[46] But I think it would be wrong to ignore the psychological influence of the dominance of laboratory experimentation and vivisection as the means of pushing back the frontiers of biological knowledge. This method which requires the researcher to distance himself from the animals he is investigating, has given powerful support to the continued belief in a radical dichotomy between man and other animals.

Within the past few years the climate of opinion has begun to change under the influence of the new science of animal ethology, in which researchers devote themselves to constant observation of how animals behave, particularly in their natural habitats. Those who participate in such research find it increasingly difficult to think of the higher animals as creatures governed entirely by instinct, or to suppose that no element of personal thought and intentionality influences their actions.[47] According to W. H. Thorpe 'no one who has worked for a long period with a higher animal such as a chimpanzee . . . is justified in doubting (their) purposiveness . . . Such purposiveness is also clear to the experienced and open-minded observer with many of the Canidae, with some, probably many, other mammals and with certain birds'.[48]

Moreover the experiment of teaching chimpanzees Ameslan, a sign-language used by the deaf and dumb, seems to show that their inability to speak has more to do with the shape of their larynx than their intelligence,[49] while their recognition of themselves in mirrors and photographs suggests an awareness of self.[50] There is some evidence that elephants cover their dead with leaves and branches which would seem to imply a conscious recognition of death.[51] And the fact that dolphins have larger and more extensively convoluted brains than we do might encourage us to be cautious in our claims for the absolute supremacy of human intelligence, at least until we know more about the workings of the cetacean nervous system,[52], and have studied more fully their patterns of behaviour and social life.

However even if we are eventually satisfied that no other creature on earth comes near the mental capacities of a healthy human adult with an undamaged brain, it remains true that the difference in intelligence between man and other animals is one of degree rather than kind. And since the human child takes so long to reach maturity, there will be stages in its development when it is outclassed in mental prowess by relatively maturer members of other species. Consequently the prevalence of infant mortality in human history would seem to exclude all theories of life after death which depend on belief in the unique value of the human consciousness. Whether these naturalistic considerations prove fatal to the whole notion of human immortality is a matter to which we must return at a later stage in our argument.

4 The Attenuation of Doctrinal Support for Belief in a Future Life

Life after death is an integral part of the traditional framework of Christian doctrine. It is not at all surprising therefore that it should suffer with other doctrines from the gradual erosion of belief in traditional Christianity which has taken place in recent centuries. Nicholas Lash pictures the contemporary theologian 'doing theology on Dover beach', and listening to the 'melancholy, long, withdrawing roar' of the 'Sea of Faith'. Consequently for Lash the future hope is a mythological fantasy, and belief in paradise equivalent to belief in fairyland.[1]

There are two reasons why the future hope is called in question by the decline in traditional orthodoxy: first because it is deprived of the support it has hitherto received from the very high evaluation of man taught in the classical doctrines of creation, incarnation and atonement; and secondly because the imagery of heaven and hell in which the future hope has been clothed is in itself particularly vulnerable to critical inquiry.

The biblical creation story is entirely geocentric and man-orientated. What God created was this earth as a place for man to live on and to exercise dominion over, with animals and plants to serve his needs, and with sun, moon and stars provided as 'lights in the sky to shine upon the earth'.[2] A slightly more sophisticated version of this was put forward in the Middle Ages according to which our earth was a globe hung in space and all the rest of the universe was confined in ten successive transparent spheres which rotated around us.[3] However, both the biblical and the mediaeval understanding of reality unite in supposing that man was at the centre of all things. As Peter Lombard put it in the 12th century, 'The Universe is made for the sake of man – that is, that it might serve him; therefore is man placed at the middle point of the Universe'.[4]

This remains the normative Christian perspective on the creation, as can be seen by consideration of the references to it in the various new services of Holy Communion which have been authorised in recent years. For example the new Roman rite declares 'you formed man in your own likeness, to his hands you entrusted the universe, so that in obedience to you, his creator, he might exercise dominion over the whole created world'.[5] And this is in no way an isolated example as the reader can discover if he chooses to consult the latest liturgies, catechisms, and popular accounts of Christian belief.[6] Galileo's inquisitors would be most unlucky to come across any affronts to their geocentric susceptibilities, if they were to return to earth in the 20th century and participate in a supposedly 'modern' form of worship. The twin beliefs that God created the universe for the sake of man, and that he created man in his own image and likeness remain firmly entrenched in the classical language of even the most modern services.[7] Clearly such doctrines imply a very high evaluation of man's worth in the sight of God, and therefore greatly increase the credibility of supposing that God would wish to sustain him in being beyond the frontiers of death.

But a still higher value is accorded to humanity by the further belief that after man had marred his divine likeness by falling into sin, God himself became man in the incarnation, and died on the cross to redeem us.[8] According to E. L. Mascall the fact that 'God has himself become man in the incarnation . . . has sealed human nature with a certificate of value whose validity can never be questioned'.[9] And Pope John-Paul II writes 'the incarnation of the Son of God emphasises the great dignity of human nature; and the mystery of redemption . . . reveals the value of every human being'.[10]

Moreover the two doctrines of incarnation and redemption not only enhance man's status by asserting that the creator of the universe literally underwent an 'at-one-ment' with man's being, but are also seen in the Christian tradition as grounds in themselves for belief in our eternal destiny. Thus for the early Fathers, God's incarnation implies our 'deification'.[11] God becomes what we are so that we might be immortal as he is.[12] So too with the doctrine of the cross described by St Gregory Nazianzus as faith in 'God put to death that we might have life'.[13]

Consequently we can see that when the central doctrines of the Christian creeds are understood in their traditional sense they form a framework in which belief in a future life has a natural place. But we can also see that when they are questioned, the future hope will also appear to be under threat. It is therefore profoundly significant that although these doctrines remain entrenched in even the newest liturgies and papal pronouncements, a growing number of Christian as well as secular writers are convinced, with Canon J. S. Bezzant that, 'known facts of astronomy, geology, biological evolution, (and other learning) . . . have banished . . . (the traditional) scheme beyond the range of credibility'.[14]

The delayed impact of the Copernican revolution is by far the most crucial element in undermining the traditional vision of man's place in the cosmos. According to Sir Bernard Lovell our galaxy contains 100,000 million stars, but our galaxy is by no means the entirety of the universe, for wherever we look in space we see similar star systems and Sir Bernard guesses that there may be between 100 and a 1000 million galaxies each containing perhaps a 100,000 million stars.[15] Professor Robert Jastrow doubles both these estimates,[16] and a television 'Horizon' programme multiplies Lovell's estimate for galaxies a hundredfold.[17] But let us take the lowest figure and assume there are 'only' 100,000 million stars in our galaxy and 'only' 100 million galaxies. Simply to be aware of these figures ought to inhibit talk of 'all of creation' being 'made for man', or of man being 'the crown and glory of all that God has made'.[18] The first is manifestly false, and the second seems highly unlikely. For if we follow the logic of the biblical creation doctrine set forth in Isaiah 45.18 that 'God did not create the earth in vain, he formed it to be inhabited', we ought to conclude that this would apply also to other planets of other stars. Indeed the fewer planets in the universe with intelligent or sentient life upon them the harder it is to believe in a wise and purposeful creator, who values life, intelligence and feeling. Yet even if we suppose that only one star in a million possesses a planet capable of sustaining intelligent life, there would still be at least ten million, million such planets in the universe.[19] And to suppose that in no case has life evolved to a higher state than man seems an incredible assumption to make, and one that does no honour to the wisdom of God.

Moreover consider the age of the universe. Estimates seem to vary between 10 and 20 thousand million years,[20] so I shall take Carl Sagan's estimate of 15,000 million years. If we then follow Sagan's example and picture this entire history compressed into a single year with the 'big bang' taking place on 1 January then our galaxy came into being on 1 May; our earth was formed on 14 September; primitive life began on 16 December; man emerged on 31 December at about 10.30 p.m.; and at 11.59.56, four-hundredths of a second before midnight on the last day of this cosmic year, Jesus Christ was born.[21] Awareness of the scale of this history seems almost inevitably to call in question Pope John-Paul II's claim that 'Jesus Christ is the centre of the universe and of history'.[22]

I accept that Don Cupitt is right to say, 'there is no reason in strict logic why this new world-view should be taken as falsifying the old religious picture of man's place in the universe. Maybe the Creator of a universe sixteen billion light-years across is primarily interested in the thoughts and deeds of human beings . . . and maybe the central event in the whole of the billions of years of cosmic history is the Creator's incarnation in Jesus of Nazareth'.[23] But as Cupitt goes on to say, ever since Giordano Bruno first spelt out the implications of belief in a plurality of worlds in 1584, many have sensed a certain incongruity about the continuation of the older picture.

Moreover although many opponents of the traditional vision have been explicitly hostile to religion, or have been theologians of a very radical stance like Don Cupitt, it should be noted that there are good religious grounds for seeking to come to terms with the new knowledge. If it is reasonable to suppose that intelligent, sentient life has developed elsewhere in the cosmos it would also seem reasonable to believe that such life forms have come into a relationship with God. If God created man for fellowship with him, one would expect this also to apply to other life forms of comparable intellectual and moral development. Our vision of God is enhanced, not diminished if we suppose that his purposes extend far more widely than simply concern for the spiritual wellbeing of our own species.

E. L. Mascall takes a different view. He argues that 'God unlike man, is not limited in his resources and has no need to be governed by considerations of economy. If he is self-existent Goodness and if *"bonum est diffusivum sui"*, may we not think of him as tossing off in the sheer joy of creation such trifles as galaxies, in vast excess of what is strictly necessary for the fulfilment of his ultimate purpose of creating man?'.[24] Yet even on Mascall's own premises this is an odd conclusion to arrive at. Starting from his assumption that God is self-existent goodness and that the good naturally wishes to pour forth itself, why should he not conclude that God's joy in creation would extend to a liberal creation of sentient intelligent beings with

whom God could relate? And as we asked earlier, what grounds
have we for supposing that God confined his purposive creation to
just one planet?

I would argue that any account of divine creation which is to be
religiously satisfying today should assume that a purposeful and
loving creator would will to create a cosmos in which sentient
rational life abounded and, evolving in numerous ways in many
planetary systems, would subsequently enter into the same relationship of love with the divine creator as the religious experience of
mankind claims that the human species has enjoyed.

It should be noted also that there is nothing in modern scientific
discoveries about the universe which precludes a doctrine of divine
creation. Indeed Professor Jastrow, Director of NASA's Institute for
Space Studies, declares that 'As a result of the most recent
discoveries we can say with a fair degree of confidence that the
world has not existed for ever; it began abruptly, without apparent
cause, in a blinding event that defies scientific explanation . . . In
science, as in the Bible, the world begins with an act of creation'.[25]
Sir Bernard Lovell agrees: 'The Universe was created . . . in their
search for the beginning the astronomers have at last scaled the final
rocky pinnacle, only to find that the theologians have been sitting
there for centuries'.[26]

One could of course quote other scientific authorities who agree
on the basic facts, but not on the theistic interpretation given to
them by Jastrow and Lovell.[27] And much philosophical work would
need to be done to establish more fully the meaning of their claims.[28]
This is not my present purpose. All I would wish to claim is that
belief in a divine creator is *compatible* with the findings of modern
astronomy. But note it is a belief in the creation of a universe vast
beyond our imagining in both space and time, and so I would
further argue that in the light of this knowledge it is hardly
reasonable to continue to suppose that the sole cause for this 'mighty
work of God's' was that on one tiny planet a species could evolve
with whom, alone of all his creatures, God could relate. On both
scientific and religious grounds such a notion ought by now to be
otiose.

But to assume that God can relate to others of his creatures raises
the question of whether or not he would seek to win their at-one-
ment with him by becoming incarnate on their planets, just as
Christian doctrine teaches he did on earth. Sidney Carter gives a
bold affirmative answer to this query in one of the very few 'post-

Copernican' hymns known to me:[29] 'Every star shall sing a carol'.
Consider the following verses:

> Who can tell what other cradle
> high above the milky way
> Still may rock the King of Heaven
> on another Christmas Day?
>
> Who can count how many crosses
> still to come or long ago
> Crucify the King of Heaven?
> Holy is the name I know.
>
> Who can tell what other body
> he will hallow for his own?
> I will praise the Son of Mary,
> brother of my blood and bone.

The difficulty with this is the sheer number of incarnations that
would be required. I noted earlier that even assuming only one
inhabitable planet per million stars we would end up with ten
million million potential worlds on which rational creatures could
evolve. In fact however, according to Professor Roland Puccetti,
there is 'a conviction growing among scientists that about 5 per cent
of all visible stars are both single – hence capable of providing stable
planetary orbits – and of the right size to create "habitable"
temperature zones for the spontaneous generation and evolution of
life'.[30] If this is so then 500,000 million million incarnations would
be necessary.

   Dr Mascall accepts that numbers of this order of magnitude are
being discussed, but suggests that even if rational corporeal beings
exist on this number of planets, it would remain possible that man
may be the only such creature to have fallen and therefore the only
one in need of redemption through a divine incarnation.[31] There are
two problems with this. First it would totally destroy the claim
which Mascall so ardently champions elsewhere[32] that divine
incarnation indicates how uniquely precious man is to God. For on
the view we are now considering all other rational corporeal
creatures would enjoy a far closer relationship, since they would
exist in a perfect state of natural at-one-ment with God, open to man
only through 'incorporation into Christ' (according to the doctrinal
system Mascall is taking for granted). Second, this whole notion of

redemption being necessary to atone for a past 'fall' from grace implies belief in an original state of perfection from which man has declined. In the light of our knowledge of evolution we know this concept to be unfounded. Consequently Christians who still wish to talk about a 'fall' usually explain the 'falleness' of man as the consequence of the continuing influence of his 'animal past'. On this basis 'falleness' would seem the inevitable condition of all rational creatures who are evolving from a 'bestial' origin.[33] Hence if there is any life at all left in such doctrinal formularies we would have to posit incarnation on all planets where rational beings were evolving.

But a concept of incarnation which would allow 'the only-begotten son of God' to become incarnate repeatedly all over the universe would evacuate the concept of all that was held to be most valuable in the traditional doctrine. The 'received' understanding of the person of Christ as expressed in St Paul's Epistle to the Colossians is that 'in him the complete being of God, by God's own choice came to dwell', or again 'in Christ the complete being of the Godhead dwells embodied'. [34] To suppose that the 'complete being of the Godhead' was simultaneously present on a million other planets would radically transform the normal sense in which these words were understood. And with 500,000 million, million worlds to 'visit'[35] in the limited timescale in which planets are inhabitable, multiple simultaneous incarnations would be inevitable! The more one tries to make sense of this picture, the more the received understanding of the doctrines of incarnation and atonement dies the death of a thousand qualifications.[36] These doctrines came into being against a back-cloth of a geocentric, man-oriented vision of the cosmos. It is hard to see how they can survive the passing of that world-view, and a psychological acceptance of a wider vision of reality.

It may seem surprising to some that I have concentrated on the erosion of the traditional system of Christian doctrine through the discoveries of modern astronomy. In theological circles it is far more common to stress the importance of other factors. Yet surveys of why young people are increasingly resistant to Christian belief show that 'modern astronomy' is repeatedly given as a reason for regarding Christianity as discredited.[37] So it seemed sensible to draw attention to this neglected, but possibly crucial factor, in the moulding of the modern secular world view.

As I have already mentioned in passing the theory of evolution has also had a significant effect in undermining the bulwarks of orthodoxy by calling in question the doctrine of an historical fall of man, and hence the need for a divine redeemer to reverse that fall. We also saw in the previous chapter that evolution has profoundly influenced man's self-understanding by revealing more fully his place in the natural order. Further, the debates about evolution in the last century served to draw the attention of the general public to the difficulties of treating the Bible as a compendium of divine oracles. Scholars had recognized this much earlier, but evolution brought the message home to a much wider audience.

Biblical criticism itself has made its own contributions to the weakening of the traditional framework of belief. For example many scholars have come to believe that the concepts of original sin and substitution atonement are more read into, than read out of the New Testament epistles.[38] And there is a widespread consensus among biblical scholars that St John's Gospel cannot be treated as an accurate record of the actual words of Jesus. Yet without the evidence of the Johannine sayings, the Gospel picture of Jesus is of a religious leader who had no conception of himself as being literally and personally God. And it is hard to think that one could actually be God incarnate and not know it![39]

The concept of divine incarnation, at least in the classical form in which it was expressed at the Council of Chalcedon of 451, has also suffered theological criticism at least since F. D. E. Schleiermacher, the so-called 'father of modern theology', published his book, *The Christian Faith* in the early 19th century. Schleiermacher asked whether it was really meaningful to think of two distinctive natures (divine and human) coming together to form one (divine) person. He also asked how far it was possible to declare that Jesus was fully human, with all the attributes of humanity and yet not *be* a human person.[40] Questions of this type have been constantly raised in the ensuing century and a half, and it is not clear that orthodoxy can give any satisfactory reply to them. Consequently there is a vigorous on-going debate about the nature of Christological language which naturally erodes confidence in the traditional doctrine.

The theory of the atonement has also been seriously attacked from the standpoint of moral philosophy. It has been asked in what sense the death of an innocent person can take away the guilt of sinners, whose conscience should be still further troubled by the notion of an innocent suffering in their place. Moreover the morality of a God who could not forgive without first demanding a sacrifice has also been raised, and this difficulty cannot be removed by postulating that God supplied the sacrifice himself, for to what purpose was it then offered?[41]

This is not the place to discuss the pros and cons of all these various criticisms of traditional orthodoxy. Our sole concern at present is to record the 'sociological' fact that such criticisms have to a very great extent eroded the confidence, even of Christian believers and theologians, in the traditional doctrines of creation, incarnation and redemption. Traditionally the grounds for belief in life after death have, in Christianity, been closely associated with these doctrines and to a considerable extent derived from them. But if we find the traditional framework to be no longer tenable, and yet still wish to take seriously the possibility of life after death, then our discussion cannot depend on an evaluation of man as a creature whom God made in his own image and likeness, whose nature God took upon himself, and who has been saved from sin and death by a divine redeemer.[42]

Moreover an even greater difficulty confronts us: namely that the contemporary Christian can draw no support from the traditional eschatological vision of his faith. Indeed the inherited beliefs about the nature of life after death, namely the doctrines of heaven and hell, so far from leading the way to a future hope, are among the greatest stumbling blocks across its path.

The traditional doctrine teaches that there will be one definitive last judgement in which the whole of mankind is separated into two groups; the saved will receive God's blessing and enter eternal life; the damned will receive his curse, and be thrown into a lake of fire and brimstone with the devil and his angels, there to be tormented day and night for ever.[43] This account which I have collated from St. Matthew's Gospel and the Book of Revelation, was taken for granted by most of the Christian tradition for almost nineteen hundred years, and instances of such teaching survive to this day. But it is open to all manner of objections.

As David Hume pointed out 'heaven and hell suppose two distinct species of men, the good and the bad; but the greatest part of mankind float betwixt vice and virtue. Were one to go round the world with an intention of giving a good supper to the righteous and a sound drubbing to the wicked, he would frequently be embarrassed in his choice, and would find the merits and demerits of most men and women scarcely amount to the value of either'.[44] In similar vein H. B. Wilson urged in his classic critique of hell; 'if we look around and regard the neutral character of the multitude we are at a loss to apply either the promises or the denunciations of revelation'.[45] On any account of human nature we would, I believe, be forced to conclude that no one is so utterly good or so spiritually mature either to deserve, or fully appreciate instant translation to a life of eternal bliss in intimate communion and fellowship with God; equally, no one is so wholly evil as to merit nothing but endless torment.

The 'Protestant' response to the first difficulty is to stress that we are 'saved' and 'fitted for heaven', not by our own merits, but solely through our reliance on the 'amazing grace' of Christ's sacrificial death for us. But if I were to be instantly 'made perfect' as this suggestion would seem to require, we would have to ask whether it was truly 'I' who had continued. For it could be argued that what had actually happened was that I, with all my imperfections, had ceased to exist, and a new perfect creature bearing some resemblance to me at my best had been created to take my place. So this solution will not do. The Catholic response is to suppose that those considered to be ultimately worthy of heaven will undergo an intermediate stage of 'purging' their sins in order to fit them for heaven. In principle there is much to be said for this suggestion, though not for the traditional view that this purgatory would consist of a long period of continuous torment. Few today believe that the simple infliction of pain is a good way to bring about moral reformation, even if a case can be made for the sharp shock of punishment to bring a person to his senses.[46] But as R. S. Peters argues 'rewards and praise for tasks reasonably done are more likely to improve performance than punishment and blame for tasks badly done'.[47] And there is considerable evidence available now to show that love, sympathy and understanding coupled with the opportunity for a person to make a fresh beginning are far more potent means to the reform or strengthening of character than any kind of purely punitive retribution.[48] However the notion of purgatory as an intermediate state for our further development and growth after death need not depend on outmoded notions of the nature of punishment, and as John Hick says, 'The gap between the individual's imperfection at the end of this life and the perfect heavenly state in which he is to participate has to be bridged; and purgatory is simply the name given in Roman theology to this bridge'.[49]

But although a modified concept of purgatory can solve the problem of our unworthiness for heaven, it does nothing to mitigate the other objection to the traditional schema, namely that no finite creature can truly be said to deserve the infinite horrors of hell.[50] As Hume says, 'Punishment, according to our conception, should bear some proportion to the offence. Why then eternal punishment for the temporary offences of so frail a creature as man?[51] Rudolf Hess as the Deputy Führer of the Third Reich must be regarded as at least partially responsible for the appalling crimes of that vile régime. Yet after he had served more than thirty years of his life-imprisonment the conscience of the western world began to clamour for his release: 'Enough is enough; no purpose is served in continuing to incarcerate that frail old man for his crimes committed so long ago.' Few civilised countries are prepared to regard a sentence of life imprisonment as binding upon the prison authorities. No matter how dreadful the offence a time will come when parole is considered and eventually release granted. Is God less merciful than we are?

The case against the traditional descriptions of both heaven and hell is that they display a lamentable lack of imaginative sensitivity. 'Eternal rest' is by far the most common description of the life of heaven, followed closely by allusions to endless services of Christian worship. But as Francis Newman commented in the last century such an existence 'is certainly too monotonous for an eternity . . . to make a new life desirable it must give us something to do, something worth striving for, and a career by which we may improve in virtue'.[52] John Hick develops this point: 'deep conceptual difficulties emerge when we try to visualise a society of perfected individuals in a totally stress-free environment from which pain, sorrow and death have been banished. The basic problem is to conceive of a worthwhile human existence in a situation in which there can be no needs, lacks, problems, perils, tasks, satisfactions, or therefore purposes'.[53] Hick notes that many of the Christian mystics have given moving descriptions of 'the beatific vision in which the finite spirit knows God directly as the ultimate reality of all being'.[54] But this would not seem an appropriate 'next' life for those of us who have little present experience of the contemplative existence. These considerations support my earlier point that heaven, as tradition-ally described, is only intelligible as an ultimate goal, rather than as a life that follows on from our present existence. Hence the Christian vision of heaven has to be supplemented by speculation about what other kind of life after death might be possible as the next stage of any supposedly ongoing existence. On its own the traditional doctrine will not suffice.

I now turn to the most dreadful aberration of the Christian

conscience, namely that the spectacle of the sufferings of the
damned will provide one of the greatest joys of the saints in heaven.
This belief, which was derived from Revelation 14.10, was given
horrific currency by Tertullian in about the year 200 A.D. 'At that
greatest of all spectacles, the last and eternal judgement, how shall I
admire, how laugh, how rejoice, how exult when I behold . . . so
many magistrates liquefying in fiercer flames than they ever kindled
against the Christians; so many sage philosophers blushing in red-hot
fires with their deluded pupils; . . . so many dancers tripping more
nimbly from anguish than ever before from applause'.[55] This belief
was, in the early period, peculiar to Tertullian. No other Christian
writer expresses such sentiments before the Middle Ages, and since
Tertullian joined the Montanist sect in protest against the supposed
leniency of the Catholic Church, his views need not have concerned
us, but for the fact that in the 12th century they were taken up by
Peter Lombard.

According to Lombard, 'the elect shall go forth . . . to see the
torments of the impious, and seeing this they will not be affected
with grief, but will be satiated with joy at the sight of the unutterable
calamity of the impious'.[56] Peter Lombard's work, *The Sentences* was
declared to be the orthodox teaching of the Catholic Church at the
Fourth Lateran Council of 1215 A.D., and throughout the Middle
Ages it served as the standard textbook of Catholic theology, not
being replaced by the *Summa* of St Thomas Aquinas (1225–1274
A.D.) until the 16th century.[57] But Aquinas too gave modified
approval to this foul doctrine for he wrote, 'in order that the
happiness of the saints may be more delightful to them and that they
may render more copious thanks to God for it, a perfect view of the
sufferings of the damned is granted to them'.[58] In fairness to St.
Thomas we should note that contrary to the view of Lombard and
Tertullian he insisted that the saints would not rejoice in the
punishment of the wicked as such, but merely at their own
deliverance from sharing such a fate.[59] But even so the notion is
appalling, not least from the supposition that God would arrange
such a display in order to enhance the gratitude of the redeemed.

Concerning the precise nature of the torments one can perhaps
give some idea of their full horror by saying that according to the
Catechism of the Council of Trent they would comprise 'an
accumulation of all punishments'.[60] To read the lurid accounts
provided in sermons and popular apologetic between the 12th and
19th centuries is to be aware of the depths of sadism to which the

human imagination can sink when it supposes itself to have divine authorisation for such exercises.[61] What is even worse, however, is that minds fed on such horrors were in some cases able to translate their imaginings into reality.

W. E. H. Lecky points out that if you tell people, 'that the Being who is the ideal of their lives, confines his affection to the members of a single Church, that he will torture for ever all who are not found within its pale, and that his children will for ever contemplate those tortures in a state of unalloyed felicity, you will prepare the way for every form of persecution'.[62] Thus Queen Mary I of England ('Bloody Mary') justified her persecution by saying: 'As the souls of heretics are hereafter to be eternally burning in hell, there can be nothing more proper than for me to imitate the Divine vengeance by burning them on earth'.[63] And precisely similar arguments were used by the officers of the Inquisition whose manuals of torture exactly mirror their descriptions of what they suppose God to have in store for the heretics after death.[64]

Because of such considerations Bertrand Russell came to believe that 'the more intense has been the religion of any period, and the more profound the dogmatic belief, the greater has been the cruelty'.[65] And Don Cupitt supports this view suggesting that the lesson of history is that at least in some periods, 'Christians became cruel men, because they believed in a cruel God'.[66] A similar argument is championed by Percy Dearmer who draws attention to the fact that although theologians in the Middle Ages studied and analysed sin with extraordinarily subtle thoroughness they scarcely ever discussed cruelty. Anger and wrath were indeed condemned, but not a word was ever said about the passionless infliction of pain. This moral blindness must have some cause. The doctrine of hell seems a plausible candidate.[67]

A further connection between belief in hell and indifference to human suffering is suggested by the evidence of novels, diaries and autobiographies concerning the strict upbringing of children in the Victorian period. Ian Bradley's detailed study of this material leads him to the conclusion that 'some of the worst cases of parental cruelty and indifference to children on the part of the Victorian middle classes were to be found in evangelical homes' where there was an 'overwhelming preoccupation with death and hell'.[68]

The case against the doctrine of hell is therefore that it is inconsistent with belief in the justice, goodness and love of God: against justice because there would seem no fair way one could

divide mankind into two wholly distinct groups, or justly punish
finite sin with infinite retribution; and against love and goodness
because it attributes limitless cruelty to God, and has inspired
appalling cruelty in man.

Modern evangelicals are acutely conscious that by all normal
standards hell is a doctrine of appalling cruelty. Thus J. A. Motyer,
principal of one of the leading Anglican Evangelical Colleges,
comments: 'The idea of eternal ruin . . . simply cannot be allowed
to continue as a possibility if there is any allowable way of escaping
from it. Every sensitive spirit will shrink from . . . the horror
involved in taking the New Testament threats of endless anguish in
what appears at first sight to be their plain meaning.'[69] Unfortunately however Motyer believes that 'the facts, in so far as they
are revealed' allow for no escape from the doctrine.[70] If Holy
Scripture teaches everlasting punishment then 'we can only seek
humbly to follow what is written for our learning',[71] in spite of the
fact that on Motyer's own admission such teaching offends against
our reason, love, sympathy and sensitivity.[72] But 'God is greater
than . . . our finite logic'[73] and 'His ways are not our ways, nor our
thoughts His thoughts'.[74]

One can only feel sympathy for a man who continues to imprison
himself inside a system of thought which horrifies his conscience. But
there are two ways he could leave his Bastille: first he could note that
the doctrine of revelation itself requires belief that the language God
uses to reveal himself should be adequate to its purpose. Consequently if God reveals himself as self-giving love, it would be as
contradictory to that central message to attribute unlovely action to
him, as in ordinary human discourse it would be contradictory to
talk of a cruel and loving person. J. S. Mill declared, 'I will call no
Being "good" who is not what I mean by "good" when I use that
word of my fellow-creatures'.[75] A person with a high doctrine of
revelation ought to be willing to make precisely the same
comment.[76]

Secondly, why should Motyer be content with what 'at first sight'
appears to be the plain meaning of the New Testament? The
consensus of New Testament scholarship, which seeks by critical
study to set Jesus' teaching in the context of first century religious
thought, is that although Jesus freely used the imagery of eternal
judgement it does not appear to have been in any way central to his
own thought.[77] For example, the parables of the sheep and the goats
and of Dives and Lazarus are manifestly set against the back-cloth of

eschatological imagery.[78] However the message which Jesus used these stories to drive home would appear to be that it is contrary to God's will for the fortunate in this life to live in pleasure completely indifferent to the sufferings of the poor and needy. Since Jesus taught his disciples to pray that God's will should be done on earth *as it is in heaven*, it seems inconceivable to suppose that he was wanting to teach that the divisions between man and man which he found so intolerable on earth would be intensified in the next world albeit with reversal of positions! One of the perils facing a teacher who uses a popular story to illustrate a point he is making is that people all too often remember the story and ignore his purpose in telling it. This seems to have happened to Jesus in these instances.

New Testament critics, generally agree that Jesus' teaching about the fatherhood of God was the most distinctive element in his thought.[79] It also appears that one very important reason for the hostility of the Scribes and Pharisees towards Jesus was that they disagreed with his teaching about the need to exhibit unlimited forgiveness to sinners. In the light of these considerations it would be strange indeed to suppose that a message of everlasting torture was an integral part of Jesus' thought.

Consequently Canon J. S. Bezzant argues that the literary and historical criticism of the Bible and the teaching of Jesus have joined hands with the moral conscience of mankind to banish the doctrine of endless torment so far beyond credibility that even a straight-forward exposition of the traditional schema sounds to con-temporary Christians like a malicious travesty of their faith.[80] For although the language of hell still lingers on, because the Christian Churches have always found it extremely hard to rid themselves of any doctrine which has once been established, there is no doubt that it has little influence today, except in some of the more conservative areas of Evangelical and Roman Catholic thought. And with regard to the Roman tradition it is noteworthy that however conservative Pope John-Paul II may be in other areas he is prepared, 'in the light of the truth that "God is love" ', to countenance 'tentatively reaching out towards some later phase in the history of salvation – not disclosed in revelation and the scriptures – which might put an end to this separation between those who are saved and those who are damned'.[81] Such a sentiment would certainly have been sufficient to secure his immolation if he had been living under the jurisdiction of the Grand Inquisitor Torquemada in the high middle ages, and coupled with his lifting of the ban on Galileo's teaching on the 26 January 1980 it shows that at least some recognition of doctrinal change is possible in even the most conservative quarters.

Let us now return to the central problem raised by this chapter, namely the extent to which the notion of life after death is affected by the attenuation of traditional orthodoxy in the secularised areas of the western world. Clearly the effect is profound in that when the whole corpus of traditional Christianity possessed men's minds, belief in life after death was simply taken for granted,[82] whereas in 1979 a survey of various 'cults of unreason' in our present society simply listed belief in life after death as one of a large number of 'fringe beliefs' to be found in our pluralistic environment.[83] There is nothing very surprising about this development because since the demise of the mediaeval Christian world-view, no alternative overall picture of reality in which life after death could be supposed to fit has gained any wide general support.

The doctrines of creation, incarnation and redemption, as well as those of heaven and hell substantially contributed to, and were in turn shaped by, the mediaeval view of man's place in the cosmos and of crime and punishment. All therefore are affected by the demise of this overall picture and, with the possible exception of the belief in hell, the attenuation of these doctrines seriously affects any present assessment of the credibility of belief in a future life.

I place the doctrine of hell in a different category for this belief has aroused moral revulsion as well as intellectual attack, and from Hume to Russell to Flew it has formed a central plank in the case against Christian belief. It is therefore probable that ever since the mediaeval world-view was superseded, the existence of the doctrine of hell has positively militated against serious consideration being given to the case for life after death.

Yet if the rational status of the belief in a future life is to some extent assisted indirectly by the decline of belief in hell, the same is emphatically not true of the attenuation of other traditional beliefs. For historically speaking, the rational grounds for belief in a future life have, in the Christian tradition, depended ultimately on the supposition that it was reasonable to think that God would wish to grant man immortality. Indeed William James in his classic study of *The Varieties of Religious Experience* found that for almost all the cases he investigated God primarily mattered as the provider of immortality.[85] And the Spanish philosopher Miguel de Unamuno made the same point on the basis of a study of all the leading thinkers of Christian history.[86]

But to believe that the omnipotent creator will wish to act directly to confer immortality on each individual human being depends upon a belief in the value of man for which some grounds need to be provided. In the past such grounds seemed to be available to all Christian believers through the faith expressed in the creeds of Christendom understood in a fairly literal and straightforward sense as guaranteeing man's supreme value to the creator of the cosmos. According to the Nicene Creed: 'Jesus Christ . . . Very God of Very God . . . By whom all things were made . . . for us men and for our salvation came down from heaven . . . and was made man'. When this could be believed in full assurance of faith man had adequate grounds for his future hope, and wherever today this faith is still held the grounds will seem as secure as ever. Yet the argument of this chapter is that the intellectual developments of the past four hundred years in astronomy, biology, biblical criticism, theology and philosophy have combined together to erode these foundations.

On any assessment, this evidence counts strongly against belief in a future life and supports the case for equating bodily death with personal extinction. On the other hand we have not yet considered the case which a reinterpreted version of Christianity might put forward on the basis of Christian experience. But it should at once be acknowledged that no reinterpreted version of Christianity can provide the straightforwardly simple kind of foundation that the traditional doctrinal system was once believed to ensure. Hence if any case for a future life is to be made out today, it will need to look for support beyond that which the Christian tradition has sought to offer in the past. I propose therefore to examine the alleged data from near-death experiences, psychical research and claimed memories of former lives. Finally it will be necessary to assess the significance of these data and explore whether any coherent picture of a future life can be given, or whether the case for extinction must necessarily remain in possession of the field.

Part Three

5 The Evidence from Near-death Experiences

Under the heading 'near-death experiences' I include two rather different sorts of data: first reports from people who have been resuscitated from a close encounter with death; and secondly reports collected from doctors and nurses about the death-bed experiences of some of their patients. Let us start by examining what it is that resuscitated persons claim to remember.

According to an editorial in the *Lancet* for 24 June 1978:

'Collected accounts volunteered by survivors . . . bear striking similarities. Amongst the experiences many have described are an initial period of distress followed by profound calm and joy; out-of-the-body experiences with the sense of watching resuscitation events from a distance; the sensation of moving rapidly down a tunnel or along a road, accompanied by a loud buzzing or ringing noise or hearing beautiful music; recognising friends and relatives who have died previously; a rapid review of pleasant incidents from throughout the life as a panoramic playback (in perhaps twelve per cent of cases); a sense of approaching a border or frontier and being sent back; and being annoyed or disappointed at having to return from such a pleasant experience – "I tried not to come back", in one patient's words. Some describe frank transcendent experiences and many state that they will never fear death again. Similar stories have been reported from the victims of accidents, falls, drowning, anaphylaxis, and cardiac or respiratory arrest'.

This summary agrees closely with the accounts given of such experiences in R. A. Moody's *Life after Life*, or J. C. Hampe's *To Die is Gain*, both of which have received substantial coverage in press, television and radio.[1] And readers familiar with their work will be able to fill out the *Lancet*'s summary by recalling their vivid anecdotes especially those relating to supposed 'out-of-the-body experiences', 'encounters' with deceased relatives and experiences of peace and joy. There seems no doubt about the basic authenticity of the experiences reported. M. A. Simpson comments dourly, 'collections of such anecdotes have been widely read, greatly overpraised and misrepresented in their promotional material and reviews'. But he agrees that 'there is indeed a range of interesting similarities among the accounts of their experiences given by [the] victims'.[2]

The question is how the data should be interpreted. Moody's publisher asserts that the reports are 'actual case histories that reveal there is life after death'.[3] Likewise for Dr Elisabeth Kubler Ross these experiences confirm that conscious awareness continues after bodily death.[4] However this view is challenged by the Editor of the *Lancet* who makes the logical point that 'only a deliberate use of obsolete definitions of death can enable one to claim that anybody has, under clinical conditions, returned to tell us what lies beyond death, for by working definition, periodically updated, death is just beyond the point from which anybody can return to tell us anything'. Professor Paul Kurtz comments, 'we have no hard evidence that the subjects had in fact died. Such proof is not impossible to obtain: rigor mortis is one sign, brain death is another'. What the accounts actually describe is 'the dying process or near-death experience, *not* death itself'.[5] In part this is simply an issue of semantics. In virtually all these cases breathing had ceased, the heart had stopped beating, and the patients showed no visible signs of life. If that is what one means by the word 'death' (and it is its meaning in common usage) then they had 'died' and therefore required 'resuscitation' (i.e. 'restoration to life') to bring them back to consciousness. On the other hand if the word 'death' is to be exclusively reserved for cases of irreversible brain damage and bodily dissolution, then no one, by definition, could simply be 'restored to life', for the only cases which could then be considered would be better described as examples of physical 'resurrection' (i.e. 'raising from the dead') and this is not the claim being made in these instances. Probably the least question-begging language to use is to talk of 'resuscitation from a near-death experience', or from a 'close encounter with death'. Manifestly all these persons were somewhere near the boundary between life and death and on which side of this border we locate them during their experience is the substantive issue with which we are concerned. We ought therefore to avoid pre-determining the outcome by a linguistic decision one way or the other, and see whether we can use neutral terminology to explore the data, subsequently deciding which description gives the clearer insight into what was actually happening.

Let us examine first the reports made by patients after resuscitation that at the moment their hearts stopped beating, they found 'themselves' outside their bodies, looking down upon the efforts being made to revive them: The sight of a doctor making ready to administer a life-saving cardiac injection is frequently the last recorded 'observation'.[6]

According to Sir Cyril Burt this phenomenon might have a quite natural explanation. A change of blood pressure in the inner ear can evoke a sensation of rising, hovering and floating in space. This can happen when a person is lying down and when something stops the flow of blood through the body. One might therefore expect that a person whose blood flow was checked by cardiac arrest would consequently suffer a change of blood pressure in his inner ear and have the sensation of rising up into the air and floating in space. Secondly people with vivid powers of optical imagery quite often visualise their own bodies 'and when (as not infrequently happens on critical occasions) the vividness approaches that of an actual sensation, they naturally assume that they have temporarily acquired the position in space from which this visual picture would be obtained'.[7] Burt describes how a patient who underwent an operation performed under spinal anaesthesia told him afterwards: 'I couldn't help wondering what I must look like to the doctors and nurses bending over my body, and then I actually saw myself lying there on the table . . . I was wide awake, because . . . I started to talk to nurse about it'.[8] The psychological phenomenon of visualising one's body as if from outside oneself becomes more common when a person is subject to serious emotional stress. According to Drs Druss and Kornfield 'a cardiac arrest is a sudden and frightening experience which calls forth a variety of defense mechanisms' and produces an intense underlying emotion of 'overwhelming anxiety'.[9] So we can postulate that the stress of cardiac arrest would cause visual hallucinations of an out-of-the body type. At the same time it seems probable that the cessation of circulation would cause blood pressure to change in the middle ear bringing about a sensation of floating in space. Taken together these two phenomena would seem to provide a full explanation of why we should expect dying people to fantasise about floating below the ceiling looking down on their unconscious bodies.

No doubt a natural explanation along these or similar lines might do justice to some of the reported cases. Garth Moore describes the case of a person who was convinced that while apparently unconscious undergoing dental treatment he had overheard a conversation between the dentist and the anaesthetist. Both assured him that his account of their alleged conversation was pure fantasy. This case is not strictly comparable to those we are considering in that the patient was neither near death, nor did he have an 'out-of-the-body' experience. But it is 'a warning against too ready an acceptance as veridical of an experience which rests solely on the belief of the person relating it'.[10] Moreover since psychiatric reports indicate that critically ill people frequently suffer from a variety of hallucinatory experiences,[11] it would be odd if their delusions did not sometimes take the form of visual hallucinations of the out-of-the-body type.

But one difficulty of applying this type of explanation to all the cases is that many of the patients are uncannily accurate in their descriptions of what was going on while they appeared to be in a state of deep unconsciousness poised on the brink between life and death. Professor Michael Sabom who has followed up many such cases comments that what is particularly notable is the 'great clarity of the patient's consciousness as he looks down at his body from outside, often observing exactly the frenzied efforts of the medical team to revive him'.[12] Dr Kubler Ross relates how people 'describe in magnificent detail the attempts to resuscitate them'[13] and J. C. Hampe gives several vivid examples of such cases.[14]

What is even more remarkable is that many descriptions accord with the claim to have viewed the events from a vantage point other than that of the body on the operating table. Dr Moody comments, 'Physicians have reported to me that they just can't understand how their patients could have described the things they did about the resuscitation efforts, unless they really were hovering just below the ceiling'.[15] Sometimes a resuscitated person describes what was going on in the rest of the ward, despite the fact that the curtains round the bed would have prevented this being visible unless the person 'seeing' all this was higher than the curtains. In one case described by Dr D. M. A. Leggett, Vice-Chancellor of the University of Surrey, a person who had an out-of-the-body experience in a dental surgery afterwards told the dentist, in support of his claim, that he had noticed two coins on top of a high cupboard in the room. The dentist subsequently 'climbed up to see what, if anything, was on top of the cupboard; there were, in fact, two pennies'.[16] C. D. Broad, R. A. Moody, J. C. Hampe, Lord Geddes and many other writers[17] give detailed examples of other cases where the victim claims to 'see' events associated with his collapse and resuscitation which simply could not have been visible from the position in which the body was lying. And in the cases where verification is possible, these reports are almost always found to be accurate.[18]

It remains perfectly plausible however to point out that anyone who had watched programmes about hospital life, or who had spent considerable time in hospital might well possess a basically accurate picture of a resuscitation unit; moreover as Sir Cyril Burt says, when our eyes are closed our picture of reality is 'readily influenced by subconscious impressions coming from the viscera, the muscles and the semi-circular canals';[19] and there is abundant evidence that ability to hear is the last faculty to be lost as we drift into deep unconsciousness. Combining these three factors it could be suggested that a patient's knowledge of the hospital set-up and of his own physical state, stimulated by subconsciously perceived sense impressions and auditory cues, might enable him to visualise a picture of what was going on which was impressively correct. When we further consider that almost all accounts are based on 'hear-say' reports which may have 'improved' in the telling it is still plausible to return a 'not-proven' verdict and insist on further evidence. This may in due course be forthcoming since the Department of Psychiatry at the University of Virginia is systematically collecting reports of such experiences, and perhaps detailed analysis of all the data may throw clearer light on the subject.[20]

Meanwhile experimental work has been begun on out-of-the-body experiences using carefully worked-out tests to try and verify claims made by some healthy individuals that they can leave their bodies at will. Volunteers are invited to sleep in research laboratories while wired up to instruments which continuously record eye-movements, blood pressure, brain rhythms and the electrical resistance of the skin. Meanwhile a box is suspended from the ceiling containing objects or numbers which are only visible from above.[21] The idea is that the volunteer should attempt during the night to will himself out-of-his body; notice and commit to memory the time on the laboratory clock; and notice and commit to memory the objects in the box. Since the box's contents are only visible from the ceiling the experiment, if successful, would tend to confirm the view that the mind can observe from a different vantage point from the body.

These experiments appear to have established that most claims to be able to will oneself out of the body are based on fantasy, since when checked through this type of test the volunteers are unable to fulfil the conditions.[22] But there have been two famous exceptions. Dr Charles Tart found a volunteer, known in the literature as Miss Z, who on the fourth night of testing, claimed to have willed herself out of her body and correctly identified a five figure number visible only from above, 25132.[23] Dr Karlis Osis has obtained even better results with a subject called Ingo Swann who during eight trial nights correctly identified all the objects in the suspended box on each occasion.[24] What is also extremely interesting is that at the times when the subjects said they were out of their bodies, the instruments to which the bodies were wired recorded absence of the rapid eye movements associated with dreaming, and the 'mean E.E.G. amplitude recorded during the out of the body condition was significantly less than during a non-out-of-the-body condition'.[25] Indeed the flattened pattern of brain waves could not be related to any known classification of brain behaviour![26]

But 'two swallows do not make a summer', and though these cases are impressive, the hundreds of failures must also be taken into account. One difficulty which these experiments highlight is that out-of-the-body claims which possess some measure of plausibility are extremely rare among healthy volunteers. On the other hand they are very common in the context of terminal illness. As Charles Tart observes 'the surest way to have an out-of the body experience is to almost die'.[27] This would suggest that tests with the dying would be far more likely to produce good results than with the living. One way this might be done, would be to paint memorable slogans or pictures on the upper surfaces of, say, the light-fittings in an intensive care unit. If a resuscitated patient subsequently described these markings it would strengthen the evidential quality of his report that he really had been looking down from above on the resuscitation attempts. Clearly the presence of markings visible only from the ceiling would in no way interfere with the urgent medical attention such patients need, and there would be no question of them being 'experimented on'. On the other hand the presence of such markings would provide some kind of yardstick against which to measure the veracity of any subsequent stories told by the resuscitated.

Susan Blackmore in her pamphlet, *Parapsychology and out-of-the-body experiences*, challenges this whole approach. The reports claim that 'something leaves the body, moves to another location and is there able to perceive'.[28] But is this intelligible? 'What could possible perceive . . . except some kind of eye? . . . If the eye is to see it must catch light. If it catches light it cannot be transparent and so it must be visible . . . However such floating eyes are not seen . . . If there is no floating eye then what perceives at the distant location? The only answer seems to be that whatever it is, it does not see by catching light as an eye would do. If it sees by some other means it . . . must be (through) extra-sensory perception (ESP)'.[29] But if we are to invoke ESP as an explanation at all, we might just as well postulate that the body on the bed uses some form of ESP, such as clairvoyance, telepathy or precognition to identify the objects in the box suspended from the ceiling.[30]

I do not see how Miss Blackmore's suggestion helps our understanding of the situation. The case against the supposition that the mind leaves the body and perceives from a different location without using the normal bodily organ of sight is that this notion would be wholly incompatible with any physicalist understanding of the mind-body relationship, and especially with our knowledge of the normal mechanisms of sense-perception. But ESP on the scale envisaged by Miss Blackmore would be at least equally incompatible with the physicalist position, as well as involving further difficulties of its own. Applying her argument to the near-death cases we would have to suppose that the deeply unconscious physical brain of a dying person is somehow able to perform feats of ESP which far transcend the abilities of all the most famous ESP experimenters in good health. Let us try and envisage what it would mean for a brain to use resources which were by definition *extra* to its sensory equipment of perception, and to succeed thereby in 'mimicking localised viewing'[31] in order to see objects outside the range of its normal viewing powers. When spelt out in full is there in fact any substantive difference between the view Miss Blackmore rejects and that which she accepts? In either terminology the self succeeds in perceiving from a different vantage point from that of the body, and once this is conceded, then talk of 'out-of-the-body experience' seems the simplest and clearest account to give of what is supposedly happening. If the self, by what ever means, is able to perceive and experience at a distance from the physical body, then it is reasonable to distinguish the self from the body. Hence if genuine perception from a different vantage point can be adequately evidenced it would seem that out-of-the-body experiences are correctly described as such. Yet of course to allow this has enormous implications for belief in a future life, as Drs Osis and Mitchell point out: 'If an out-of-the-body experience literally is what the term implies, that is that some part of personality is temporarily out of the body, then it would be of utmost importance for research in survival after death. If there is something in us which can get out, perceive and act apart from the body, this indeed would make it more plausible that one might also get out at the time of death and continue to exist in one way or another'.[32] (Osis and Mitchell are perhaps overstating the case in that evidence for action is inadequate, but with this proviso their argument seems sound.)

Near-death experiences are therefore of the utmost importance to research in life after death, for the evidential features in the reports made by resuscitated persons about their supposed observations provide some of the strongest grounds for supposing that the separation of the self from the body is possible.

A second evidential feature is that those to whom this experience happens become absolutely convinced of the reality of life after death no matter what their previous views were. According to R. A. Moody, 'after his experience a person no longer entertains any doubts about his survival of bodily death. It is no longer merely an abstract possibility to him, but a fact of his experience'.[33] Dr E. Kubler Ross writes, 'Not one of the patients who's had this experience was ever again afraid to die. Not one of them, in all our cases'.[34] Moreover after watching hundreds of people undergo such experiences over two decades Dr Ross found her own ideas changing. 'Before I started working with the dying, I did not believe in a life after death. Now I believe in one beyond a shadow of a doubt'.[35] John Davy too calls attention to the utter certainty of those who had near-death experiences concerning both its objective character and its profound significance for their lives. He writes:

'These experiences are for those involved as indubitable, or more so, as those in daily life'. Any attempt to explain away the experience by postulating a physiological or psychological account of them 'is to the patients concerned mere incantation. They may keep their experiences to themselves, but privately they regard such explanations as mere contortions, as unconvincing as most of us would regard the arguments of a solipsist philosopher who explains that the door in which I have just pinched my finger is only an idea in my mind. Furthermore, doctors who are prepared to take note of such experiences, especially those with a "transcendent" dimension, report a consistent and profound change in the attitude to death. The majority of these patients bring back with them an absolute certainty that their eventual physical death will simply be the entry into a mode of further existence that they have already glimpsed. These glimpses are almost always accompanied by a joy and certainty scarcely comparable to anything in ordinary life'.[36]

It is of course true that profound convictions can be based on delusory evidence and that a person's psychological sense of certainty is no necessary guide to the correctness of his views. And it will be important for us later to look carefully at the suggestions made by competent medical and psychiatric sources about the possible origin of these distinctive experiences. Meanwhile let us simply note that the data of reported human experience will always be an important contributing factor to our understanding of reality, and we need to give particularly serious consideration to experiences which decisively change the beliefs and attitudes of those who have enjoyed them.[37]

Let us now turn to another element in the characteristic 'near-death experience' namely the reported visions of deceased relatives and friends and of religious figures allegedly 'welcoming' the dying into the life beyond. Clearly these visions are hallucinatory in form and, at least in part, must reflect the religious and psychological expectations of the dying. In the case of adults one might well be tempted to dismiss such reports altogether as of no possible evidential value. But the case becomes more complicated in the case of little children. Dr G. Kliman writes, 'We should make it clear that children up to the age of ten cannot very well understand the concept of death. And the idea of the permanence of death may be as incomprehensible as the idea of infinity'.[38] Moreover in the normal course of nature most of the closest relatives and friends of young children are still alive. We know too that in times of stress children frequently hallucinate images of their parents, to whom their thoughts naturally turn for protection.

Dr Kubler Ross works with dying children, many of whom have undergone near-death experiences which they have described to her. She finds it very significant that 'in all these years that we've collected cases . . . not one of these children who nearly died has ever seen mommy and daddy, unless their parents had preceded them in death'.[39] Instead the children's visions are exclusively limited to deceased relatives, many of whom they scarcely knew, or to a religious figure like Jesus about whom they had been told. She suggests that this is a strong indication of the evidential quality of these visions, because since children cannot understand death they would not know about confining their visions to the departed, but under psychological stress would see their parents.

This argument will not do. Although children may not understand the full implications of what the word 'death' means, it is perfectly reasonable to suppose that a child can attach meaning to a parental 'explanation' that the reason Granny is no longer around is that Granny has died and gone to live with Jesus. If the child then learns that he too is dying it would be only natural that he should anticipate in his mind a future life with Granny and with Jesus, with whom Granny is apparently now living.[40]

A more substantial form of Kubler Ross' argument however is the claim that in some cases children report having been 'met' by relatives whom they did not know, but subsequently correctly described to their bewildered parents. Dr Ross gives the example of a girl met by a brother who had died before she was born and of whose existence the parents had never told her.[41] Dr Thomas Smith, writing in the GP's weekly paper *Pulse* reports the case of a child met by her grandfather's mother of whom she had had no previous knowledge, but whose photograph she recognised with great enthusiasm when first visiting an uncle's home some time after her recovery. Apparently she had never seen that photo before, nor did any other member of the family possess a photograph of this long departed relative.[42] If one can accept such testimony, this would indeed be evidence for assigning some kind of objective validity to such accounts. But one's credulity is strained at this point. For it seems remarkably fortuitous that the deceased's self-image, which we are to suppose was communicated to the mind of the child, happened to match an extant photograph taken at one particular stage in her earthly existence.

Fewer problems arise with another type of 'evidential' vision described by Sir William Barrett, FRS. He writes of 'instances where the dying person was unaware of the previous death of the spirit form he sees, and is therefore astonished to find in the vision of his or her deceased relatives, one whom the percipient believes to be still on earth'.[43] Barrett gives eight examples of such cases and Kubler Ross and Allen Spraggett each add another instance.[44] Dr Ross' case is especially striking since no one at the hospital knew at the time of the vision that the subject of it had died, since his death had occurred only an hour earlier in a traffic accident. Clearly in the context of visions where only the deceased are seen, the reliability of such reports is enhanced when it is established beyond doubt that the percipient had no knowledge that one of those he saw was in that category.

In the light of the discussion so far I conclude that a *prima facie* case exists for treating near-death experiences as evidence for the possibility of personal survival of bodily death. But at this point we must look at the medical and psychiatric background to these cases. Any person hovering between life and death must be suffering profound physical and psychological stress. A brain starved of oxygen, drugged by hallucinatory pain-killers, or excited by fever, is hardly likely to function properly and who knows what visions could be accounted for by its disturbed condition?

One key element in this discussion must be a study of the immediate consequences of heart-failure. We have already seen that checking the flow of blood throughbout the body would change the pressure in the middle ear and thus account for the sensation of floating out-of-the-body. Heart-failure would also lead to the cutting off of the brain's blood supply causing oxygen starvation to commence, which without immediate resuscitation would lead fairly rapidly to irreversible brain damage. The first results of oxygen starvation however would be to cause a paroxysmal temporal lobe disturbance. According to Dr James McHarg this would bring about mood changes in the direction of ecstasy and cause visual hallucinations with a religious other worldly colouring.[45] Clearly this would closely correspond to most of the experiences described.

Likewise many medically accepted drugs used to control pain in the final stages of terminal illness have delusional and hallucinatory effects. This is especially true of the drug ketamine (or cyclohexanone) which is an intravenously injected anaesthetic.[46] According to Dr R. A. Moody it has side effects which closely resemble out-of-the-body experiences and its after-effects include hallucinations or very vivid dreams. Other drugs such as the anaesthetic nitrous oxide, or even LSD used to control terminal pain[47] seriously affect the person's mental and psychological equilibrium.

In addition to these medical factors we must also note the psychiatric evidence presented by Dr Russell Noyes which seeks to explain the near-death experiences as a natural psychological response to the crisis of impending death. He describes them all as the product of 'depersonalisation in the face of the life-threatening danger'. [48] Noyes' claim is that death threatens all that we are, and it is only natural that the acute stress of this situation would evoke psychological defence mechanisms to shield us from having to face the reality of our own final end. One of these psychological defence mechanisms is the attempt to dissociate our self-hood from the dying body. Noyes comments 'a curious splitting of the self from its bodily representation may occur. Commonly referred to as "out-of-the-body" . . . this splitting represents an interesting negation of death . . . The threat of death is reduced to a threat of bodily annihilation . . . '. By this means, 'the reality of death is excluded from consciousness'.[49] As death draws nearer, life 'arises to a sharper focus'; 'memories of deceased persons' become 'quite clear and of such intensity as to resemble perception'; and the person rapidly reviews his whole life. This leads to a feeling of self-transcendence and ends with a 'mystical state of consciousness'.[50] The central assumption of Noyes' argument therefore is that near-death experiences can all be explained in terms of a psychological defence mechanism in order to escape from the acute anxiety and stress of recognising our impending mortality. And this argument is precisely that used by M. A. Simpson who talks of a variety of well-recognised defence mechanisms producing these phenomena.[51]

How plausible is the suggestion that near-death experiences could be accounted for by some suitable blend of physiological and psychological factors influencing the minds of the dying at a critical stage? To test this let us consider a massively documented survey of deathbed experiences compiled by K. Osis and E. Haraldsson and published in two parts, a pilot study called *Death-bed observations by physicians and nurses*, and a major work entitled *At the Hour of Death*. Their data differ from those used by Moody, Hampe and Ross in that the reports came from observers of the last moments of the dying, and not from individuals who recovered from apparent death. But there are striking similarities between the two categories because many of the dying claimed to see deceased relatives 'welcoming' them into the next world just before they actually died.

Osis and Haraldsson based their research on questionnaires completed by over two thousand doctors and nurses in the USA and India about the experiences of their dying patients. The advantage of this procedure was that it ensured that all the data came from trained medical personnel who were in a position to relate any claimed deathbed visions to the known bio-medical and psychological state of the patient, who were familiar with the problems of the critically ill, and who could describe the experiences of their patients in a standard manner so that these could form the basis for detailed computer analysis of the various factors.[52]

If, for example, deathbed visions were the product of such factors as oxygen deprivation,[53] malfunctioning of the central nervous system,[54] fever, or hallucinatory pain-killing drugs,[55] then deathbed visions could be expected to be most prevalent when such medical conditions were realised; but no such correlations were found. Similarly if the visions were the product of particular psychological states, or reflected the patient's expectations of death or recovery, then those factors also could be monitored. Once more, no significant correlations could be established.[56] Of course when the dying patient was under the influence of a medical condition, drug or psychological state which normally causes hallucinations or a feeling of disassociation, he would be as disorientated by it as anyone else would be, if not more so. But the doctors concerned seem to have found no difficulty in distinguishing between such 'normal' aberrations and the distinctive features of the specifically near-death experience. For example hallucinations which followed from a specific medical condition were normally of people still living, whereas hallucinations in the near-death situation were invariably of deceased persons.[57] The patients were all critically ill of course, and to this extent shared a common condition. Nevertheless one might have expected particular features like oxygen deprivation or stress to have had an influence on the occurrence or non-occurrence of deathbed visions, but no correlations were found even in these two instances.[58]

In short what Osis and Haraldsson's research has established is that all theories which seek to 'explain away' near-death experiences as the product of particular physiological or psychological states break down when one actually looks at the medical records of the people involved. The theories of Noyes or Simpson are shown to be based on speculation alone and to lack any kind of substantive basis.

Throughout all the discussion I have been writing of 'near-death experiences'. It should however be mentioned that although the class of material seems to be a distinctive body of data, only 15 per cent of people who are resuscitated have a story to tell about their experiences.[59] Yet doctors actually present in resuscitation wards report that psychological testing of other patients reveals them to have undergone a wide variety of vivid dreams, hallucinations, nightmares and delusions. Indeed the editorial in the *Lancet* which I cited at the beginning of this chapter points out that apart from the type of experiences familiarised by Moody and Hampe, resuscitated patients may suffer experiences of a wholly different kind. Thus 'of male survivors of cardiac arrest, 80 per cent had dreams of violence, death and aggression, such as being run over by a wheelchair, violent accidents, and shooting their way out of hospital only to be killed by a nurse . . . other patients show frank hallucinations and delusions, such as maintaining . . . that they have been in another ward all along, or describing non-existent visits home'. Then there is the 'I am dead' syndrome in which 'survivors of cardiac arrest may for some days claim that they are already dead' and indeed may undergo 'disturbing fantasies about death'.[60]

We must therefore ask whether there are grounds for supposing that the so-called near-death experiences are of any more significance than other fantasies of the critically ill. Dr Maurice Rawlings does not think they are. His book, *Beyond Death's Door*, treats the nightmares experienced by his patients during their operations as being just as significant as any visionary experiences they may subsequently describe. This is rather hard to justify because the survivors of near-death experiences themselves sharply differentiate their 'other wordly visions' from the various dreams and hallucinations some of them also experienced during their illnesses. None of them seems in any doubt that the two types of experience fall into two wholly distinct categories. Dreams, no matter how vivid, lifelike or disturbing, will quickly fade from consciousness, unless deliberately recalled and committed to memory at the moment of waking. Real experiences of a vivid kind are, by contrast, normally remembered. The evidence seems to be that dreams and delusions undergone while under anaesthetic or cardiac arrest can be reported on awakening, but are not remembered the following day. By contrast the supposed glimpses of a future life are permanently remembered and treasured. Even Dr Rawlings' key witness makes this distinction. He has no memory whatever of a nightmare of hell he told Rawlings about during one resuscitation, yet he vividly recalls a vision of his deceased mother and the joy and peace he felt during another close brush with death.[61] According to J. C. Hampe a near-death experience 'cannot be confused with a dream, because it possesses a closeness to reality which dreams never attain. In this experience, as it comes to the dying it is not a question of ideas being lived as they are in a dream; on the contrary it is life that is being thought and experienced. Above all the consciousness of the self is completely different in kind from what it is when dreaming'.[62] In the light of this, and taking into account the impact near-death experiences have on those who undergo them I suggest they have as much right to be taken seriously as any religious vision or conversion experience which profoundly changes the course of an individual's life.

This reference to religious vision raises the question of how far the near-death experiences are the product of the expectations and beliefs of the percipients. Dr Simpson hints at this in his demand for 'better studies with more careful and less biased collection and interpretation of the data . . . and with cross cultural comparisons . . . to improve our understanding of this data'.[63] However important cross-cultural data are already available. One useful survey by Dean Shiels consists of an investigation into beliefs about out-of-the-body experiences in the world's primitive cultures.[64] This research showed that at least sixty-four out of the sixty-seven cultures surveyed believe in the reality of out-of-the-body states. Conventional theories which have been put forward as explanations of out-of-the-body beliefs (social control, crisis, or dreams), were tested and found not to apply in these cultures. Hence Shiels suggests that the specificity and generality of this belief is simply a response to a genuine event; i.e. the actual occurrence of out-of-the-body experience. 'When different cultures at different times and in different places arrive at the same or a very similar out-of-the-body belief we begin to wonder if this results from a common experience of this happening'.[65]

On the wider issue of the near-death experience as such, the detailed analysis of the data in Osis and Haraldsson's survey shows a remarkable cross-cultural consensus between their respondents in both India and the USA. For although the visions of the next world were inevitably coloured to some extent by the patient's cultural and religious background, the similarities were much more striking than the differences. It seems that men and women, young and old, educated and illiterate, religious and non-religious, American and Indian, Christian and Hindu, all enjoyed essentially the same types of experience. Moreover, the other-worldly visions did not accord with the traditional belief-systems of either Christianity or Hinduism about the nature of life after death, nor did they accord with western secular assumptions of no such other world existing. All these factors seem to point to the difficulty of accounting for such experiences as projections of the patients' desires or expectations.

Some element of projection must of course be present, for the percipients often claim to see not only departed relatives and friends, but also religious figures from their own particular traditions. Evangelicals often 'see' Jesus, Catholics 'see' Mary, saints or angels, while Hindus 'see' Yama the god of death or other Hindu deities and atheists simply talk of a 'being of light'. But whatever 'entity' is seen it appears to fulfil a similar role and is evidently an important part of many near-death experiences. If there is any sense in talking of 'the religious experience of mankind' one might perhaps expect that any manifestation of the Divine presence would be interpreted within the religious and cultural tradition of the percipient. The problem in the cases we are considering is no different in kind from the general issue of relating descriptions of religious experiences arising in different faiths. And Osis and Haraldsson's central point about the universality of near-death experiences has been confirmed by more recent findings concerning the deathbed visions of Sikhs and Muslims.[66]

Near-death experiences therefore appear to confront us with data which support the possibility of personal survival of bodily death, and which cannot be accounted for by the physiological or psychological state of the patient, nor by his cultural or religious background. But this conclusion depends upon treating the reports of people like Moody, Kubler Ross, Osis and Haraldsson as reliable testimony. Is this valid? Up to a point of course the data are undeniable. No one doubts that some dying people have weird experiences. The *Lancet*, the *Journal of Psychiatry*, the International Committee for the Scientific Investigation of the Paranormal, as well as Drs. Noyes and Simpson would all agree that some resuscitated people felt as if they had gone out of their bodies, and also experienced a variety of hallucinatory images. But if we wish to claim that the dying not only had the feeling of being out of their bodies but actually did go out of them, and that they not merely had hallucinations but had hallucinations which could be supposed to possess some veridical origin external to the percipient, then we move outside the area of agreement. The case for doing so depends at least partly on whether or not we feel that the additional information vouched for by researchers like Moody and Ross is reliable. But is their witness to be trusted?

It has to be acknowledged that with regard to each of the authors there is at least some ground for suspicion. Dr Moody's research is based primarily on a hundred-and-fifty cases he has personally investigated. We have no means of checking how fairly he has presented this information, but in his second book, *Reflections on Life after Life*, Moody cites a 'return from the dead story' from Bede's *History of the English Church and People* which, according to Moody, 'resembles in many respects those heard today'.[67] However a comparison of Moody's quotation with the original text shows that Moody has made Bede's story fit his scheme, by the simple expedient of omitting all the copious data in Bede which conflict with it. Bede's account seems primarily concerned to describe the torments of hell,[68] but these are not even mentioned in Moody's version of it. If this case, which is of course the only one readily available for public checking, is a typical example of the way Moody handles his material then this casts serious doubt on his reliability.

What of Dr Kubler Ross, the doyen of all researchers in this area, whose imprimatur in the form of a foreword is sought by all her fellows?[67] Her international reputation is built on the tremendous impact of her major work *On Death and Dying* which is solely devoted to the proper treatment of the terminally ill. Her contribution to the study of near-death experience is confined to occasional articles and interviews on press and radio. No one can dispute that she has done more than anyone else to improve the care of the dying in the USA, but this does not exempt her work from possible criticism. Walter Kaufmann in an article entitled 'On death and lying' has shown that on occasion 'she makes totally unsupported claims with an air of absolute certainty'.[70] And her credibility is also called in question by noting how much of the paranormal she is prepared to vouch for. Thus she not only cites evidence of near-death experiences, but also says she has talked with a ghost and persuaded the ghost to write a letter which she has framed on her wall.[71] But that I can't believe. Such a report is not merely contrary to nature, but also contrary to all that the Society for Psychical Research has discovered in its investigations of 1684 cases of alleged apparitions. Whatever we are to make of such phenomena, one thing is common to all cases ever investigated by the SPR: 'apparitions leave no physical traces behind them'.[72] Yet if I doubt Dr Ross' veracity on this point, why should I trust her in the rest of her testimony?

This latter problem affects all the other writers I cite: Osis and Haraldsson, Hampe, Spraggett, Ebon, Fiore and Landsburg, Grof and Halifax and most of Crookall's correspondents are all prepared to endorse alleged para-normal phenomena which lie beyond my own personal 'threshold of credulity'. All would agree that a line has to be drawn somewhere, yet once one steps outside the generally agreed limits of a naturalistic world-view, there is no self-evident place at which to draw it.

Despite such doubts I cannot merely brush the data aside. Archbishop Richard Whately once wrote: 'When many coincide in their testimony (where no previous concert can have taken place) the probability resulting from this concurrence does not rest on the supposed veracity of each considered separately, but on the improbability of such agreement taking place by chance . . . For the chances would be infinite against their all agreeing in the same falsehood'.[73] In Osis and Haraldsson's survey, the data were collected by two thousand doctors and nurses in America and India; J. C. Hampe's research was done in Germany, and quite independently Drs R. A. Moody and E. K. Ross have each collected hundreds of American cases. More recently, a bibliography of books and articles relevant to near-death experiences has been published, listing two and a half thousand titles.[74] So one is dealing with a very widespread phenomenon. Moreover, such experiences seem to be far more common than even the published literature suggests, for both Dr Moody and Dr Kubler Ross have commented that whenever they give a talk on the subject at least one member of the audience comes forward with a further case, as I myself have also found when speaking on this subject.[75] This latter consideration is in the end decisive for my own attitude. Whatever doubts I may have about the methodology of other researchers, I do at least know what I myself have been told at first hand by people I trust, who have had a near-death experience themselves. In all cases such evidence broadly fits into the outlines described by other writers. And therefore, despite the considerations mentioned earlier, it seems reasonable for me to accept the general veracity of their reports.

If we accept these 'travellers' tales' from the dying as evidential, what conclusions follow? My own view is that if these experiences cannot be related to the particular nature of the patient's terminal illness, nor to his psychological state, cultural background or religious beliefs, and if no other plausible explanation can be put forward, then we have some grounds for accepting them as being what their percipients claim them to be –reports of what actually happens at the moment of death. And what appears to happen is that the soul leaves the body and begins to move on to another mode of existence. Out-of-the-body experiences support belief in the first of these stages, and while there is no direct evidence for the second, (because all our witnesses were 'recalled' before reaching it), it is at least relevant to record the absolute conviction of all the resuscitated that, had they not been brought back, that would indeed have been their destiny.

There is therefore at least some evidence to support the belief in the immortality of the self through bodily death. How, if at all, it may be possible for us to accommodate such data within our overall picture of reality, is a matter to which we must return in our final chapter.

6 The Evidence from Psychical Research

The significance of psychical research is that it appears to provide a substantial body of evidence which calls into question some of the pre-suppositions, or as C. D. Broad calls them, 'the basic limiting principles'[1] of the naturalistic world-view normally taken for granted in modern societies. Broad gives four examples of such presuppositions namely: that thoughts cannot pass from one person to another without some of the sensory equipment of both being called into play at some stage; that a person cannot have any non-inferential knowledge of the future; that our volitions can only *directly* influence the movements of our own bodies; and that when a person's body dies, his consciousness either ceases altogether, or at any rate, ceases to be able to manifest itself in any way to those still living on earth.[2] Our present concern is primarily with the first and last of these presuppositions, but in fact the validation of any claim to extra-sensory perception or influence would serve to undermine the authority of all such limiting principles.

In an earlier work I argued that there was now abundant evidence for believing both that telepathy is a reality, and that it cannot be incorporated into a materialist world-view.[3] I shall not rehearse the case here except to say that, in the years since I completed the research for that book, the case for extra-sensory perception has grown much stronger.

First, Professor C. E. M. Hansel's 'hatchet-job' on ESP (*ESP a scientific evaluation*) has itself been demolished. Hansel's case depended on showing that the key experimenters might have rigged their results. To do this he relied on an analysis of their work made by Dr G. R. Price for the journal, *Science* in 1955.[4] But in January 1972 Dr Price wrote a letter to that journal confessing that his earlier work had been based on inadequate information, was 'highly unfair' to the experimenters he had falsely accused, and after seventeen years he wished to put the record straight.[5] So the work of

Drs Rhine and Soal has been 're-habilitated' and the rug pulled from under Hansel's feet.

Moreover in recent years a 'consistent scorer' has at last been found who can be tested repeatedly in laboratory trials for ESP ability. For twelve years Pavel Stepanek delighted parapsychologists by choosing correctly between two targets approximately 55 per cent of the time instead of the 50 per cent success rate chance would have predicted.[6] This most utterly boring and in a sense, trivial 'ability' has the advantage of lending itself to statistical evaluation under controlled conditions in endlessly repeated experiments in research laboratories. And statisticians believe that this marginal improvement on chance when sustained over tens of thousands of tests during more than a decade demonstrates ESP beyond dispute.[7] So although in one sense the Stepanek experiments seem banal and pointless, and demonstrate no worthwhile or usable ESP qualities, they nevertheless are sufficient to call in question the naturalistic world-view under which such an inexplicable variation from chance ought not to happen.

However for the purposes of our present discussion earlier ESP research which concentrated on the phenomenon of telepathy is of greater significance. In my former book I discussed the evidence for telepathy emphasising Professor L. L. Vasiliev's *Experiments in Mental Suggestion* which involved the telepathic transmission of simple commands to hypnotised subjects.[8] I also stressed the number of eminent persons and societies who have participated in telepathic experiments.[9] Both the quality and quantity of evidence for this phenomenon now force its opponents into desperate straits to deny its reality. As Dr Welman comments: 'If the only answer to the vast amount of solid experimental evidence is incompetence or fraud on a global scale by men with credentials equal to those of their scientific peers, working in academic surroundings, and whose work extends historically in time over at least three generations, then the adherents of this position would seem to have adopted a stance that is even more difficult to defend than the psi hypothesis'.[10]

Yet to accept the reality of psychical phenomena requires a very considerable break with the prevailing monistic naturalism. Keith Campbell offered a large hostage to fortune when he declared, 'if even a single example of para-normal phenomena is genuine, central state materialism is false';[11] for it seems that not one, but many examples are now available. And though at some stage in the future men may reframe their naturalism to embrace psychic phenomena, this in no way alters the fact that such data are incompatible with present day materialism, and strongly favour a dualist account of man's being. Since the discrediting of a dualist doctrine of man makes most theories of a future life unthinkable,[12] the *prima facie* support for dualism which psychical phenomena provide is of great importance.[13]

But any vindication of psychical research in general and of telepathy in particular has an even greater potential significance for life after death research than just the support it gives to dualism. For if the evidence for telepathy shows that thoughts can, on occasion, pass from one mind to another without the use of the neural pathways of the brain, it provides a possible channel for communication between the living and the dead. For if mental life continues in being after bodily death the only way it could manifest itself to an embodied person would be through a telepathically communicated message. R. H. Thouless writes, 'no other person can know directly whether x's consciousness has or has not continued after the death of x. It may however be verified indirectly in communications ostensibly from him, received after death. Such identification may be taken as indirect evidence that x's stream of consciousness is going on after his death'.[14]

But do the dead ever communicate with the living? Osis and Haraldsson write, 'Spontaneous experiences of contact with the dead are surprisingly widespread. In a national opinion poll . . . twenty-seven per cent of the American population said that they had . . . widows and widowers . . . reported encounters with their dead spouses twice as often – 51 per cent'.[15] Moreover such surveys have not been confined to the USA. Similar results have been obtained in mid-Wales, south-east London, Tokyo,[16] and also in Iceland.[17]

Nor can all claims to have had contact with a lost loved-one be written off as illusory, an hallucinatory consolation prize conjured up by the grieving mind to soothe its hurt. For there have been studies to show that in some cases, there are features of the hallucination which warrant its being counted as 'veridical' rather than 'delusionary' or 'subjective'. The classic survey is G. N. M. Tyrrell's analysis of an SPR 'Census of Hallucinations', in which he was particularly interested in cases where 'a person had a waking hallucination of a recognised friend at precisely the time when that friend died'.[18] He builds up a case to show that the chances of having such an hallucination, if there were no direct link between its occurrence and the friend's death, is very much more remote than is the *de facto* incidence of such reports.[19] Moreover where details of the hallucination can be verified independently we have even stronger grounds for supposing that the hallucination is not solely the product of the percipient's mind. Myers, for example cites the case of 'Archdeacon Farler, who twice during one night saw the dripping figure of a friend who, as it turned out, had drowned during the previous day'.[20]

An even stronger case could be made if it could be shown that an apparition had communicated veridical information to the percipient which only the dead person had known. Cases like this have been cited since at least the time of St Augustine in the fourth century.[21] The classic modern case is that of James L. Chaffin who died in North Carolina in 1921, apparently leaving his farm and all his property to his third son under a will dated 1905. His wife and three other children received nothing. However four years after Chaffin's death, the inheriting son also died leaving the property to his widow and son. At this point Chaffin senior appeared to his second son, and told him where a later will could be found dividing the property equally between his four children. The will was found where indicated, proved in the law courts, and implemented. The son to whom the father appeared declared, 'We never heard of the existence of the [later] will till the visitation from my father's spirit'.[22] This case is often cited, partly because all the details of it were thoroughly investigated and recorded in a court of law, and partly because the importance of the matter to those concerned in it lends credibility to the second son's testimony of his earlier ignorance. In other circumstances one would have been more ready to interpret the apparition as a vivid calling to mind of a forgotten memory of the father in his life-time telling his son where his will could be found. But where what was at stake was the inheritance of the entire family estate it is hard to think of any son forgetting so vital a piece of information! This consideration lends support to the view that his apparition was veridical.

Some people believe that direct contact with the dead can be achieved through mediums who allegedly have the ability, while in a state of trance, to transmit messages between the dead and the living. Belief in the reality of such communications is the life-blood of the Spiritualist Churches, and mourners who consult mediums are often impressed by the convincing descriptions of departed loved-ones which the mediums give. On occasion a medium may also show knowledge of the deceased's former life. However, there are serious grounds for questioning the evidential value of these descriptions for detailed examination of these cases shows that acute observation, and intelligent guesswork would explain much of their success. Mrs Leonard was one of the most famous mediums of all time, and her work brought great comfort to many sorrowing relatives of persons killed in the First World War, who believed that she was genuinely in touch with their lost sons, whom she described in detail. However although Mrs Leonard's descriptions were thought to be so accurate, a research officer of the Society for Psychical Research found that at the first fourteen seances he listened in to, bereaved relatives were all given essentially the same description. Evidently Mrs Leonard had 'developed a model of the average young British officer as remembered by the average mother'.[23] It transpired from further seances that equally stock descriptions of elderly ladies were available for those who disclaimed all personal knowledge of deceased soldiers. This investigation brings home just how little descriptive accuracy is needed to convince mourning relatives that the medium is indeed in touch with their dead.

The presentation of accurate knowledge of events in the life of the deceased cannot always be accounted for by intelligent guesswork cued by the responses of the inquiring relative. In some cases telepathic ability must be presumed to exist in order for this knowledge to be acquired by the medium. But any knowledge of the deceased which the sitter found impressive would normally be present in the sitter's memory, albeit the unconscious memory, and telepathy from the sitter to the medium would seem to explain almost all cases.[24] Such an explanation would seem confirmed by the experience of Rosalind Heywood: 'Soon after the Second World War I decided to test a medium by having an anonymous sitting with her and mentally asking the fate of a German friend, of whom I had heard nothing since 1938 . . . I feared he must have been killed. He soon appeared to turn up at the sitting, gave his Christian name and spoke through the medium in character and reminded me of various pleasant experiences which he had shared with my family . . . He then said he had been killed in grim circumstances. *After* the sitting I made inquiries about his fate . . . He was eventually traced to a neutral country . . . where he was happily living . . . Here, then it looks as if the medium . . . was building a picture of the German from my subconscious memories and my fears as to his fate'.[25]

I suggest that an explanation of this sort would cover at least the vast majority of cases of alleged communication with the dead through mediums. The mode of contact between the living and the dead would have to have a channel at least akin to telepathy and virtually all cases of spontaneous telepathy or of spontaneous apparitions of the departed occur between people who are very close to each other either through family relationship or friendship. It must therefore always seem intrinsically improbable that a medium could on demand establish telepathic rapport with a deceased stranger, at least in comparison with the likelihood of the medium making such a contact with the person sitting with her. In almost all cases therefore the sitter, rather than the deceased, would seem the more likely source of the apparent information. It is therefore very hard to see how any reports arising from mediumship could ever be decisively established as coming from the dead rather than the living.

All the pioneers of psychical research came to realise this problem. For decades F. W. H. Myers, Henry Sidgwick and Edmund Gurney gathered data on apparitions and investigated the claims of mediums. Yet their findings seemed distinctly unsatisfying. It became clear to them that most mediums were charlatans and that even though some evidence from genuine mediums seemed quite strong one could never rule out the possibility of alternative explanations of how the mediums acquired their knowledge. Consequently all three of them died aware of the fact that their work had failed in its purpose of demonstrating the truth of the survival hypothesis to which they were committed. Myers died in 1901 leaving the unfinished manuscript of his two-volume work *Human personality and its survival of bodily death* still awaiting the key evidence. His son published the work in 1903 but Myers died conscious that it did not answer his purpose.

At this point however the most dramatic evidence for life after death begins to emerge. For Myers had resolved in advance that if he discovered that he *had* survived death after all, he would do all in his power to provide his successors in the Society for Psychical Research with the sort of evidence that would prove it. Mrs A. W. Verrall, a lecturer in Classics at Newnham College, Cambridge, decided to try and enable Myers to demonstrate his survival of death through automatic writing done by herself. Her daughter

Helen also began automatic writing and it was noticed that before she had seen her mother's scripts she was referring to the same subjects. Almost simultaneously Mrs Piper, a medium in America began to 'receive' messages purporting to come from Myers and it was resolved that they would each send their scripts independently to the Society for Psychical Research. A few years later, Mrs Fleming in India began to undertake automatic writing and she too sent her scripts to the SPR. From 1905 onwards Gurney and Sidgwick supposedly began to join Myers in attempting to 'prove' their survival, and in due course about a dozen people were involved in automatic writing which seemed to show that all three were attempting to send messages. Later, it seemed that Dr A. W. Verrall (d. 1912) and Professor Henry Butcher (d. 1910) had also joined in the attempts to send messages back to the living.[26]

To ease exposition, I will describe what happened as if Myers *et al.* really were sending messages back, since to preface every remark with 'it seems as if' would be extremely tedious. I do not intend any question-begging here – the case must be judged on its merits.

The way Myers and the others attempted to prove their survival was to send incomplete and partial messages to a variety of respondents. Taken in isolation each individual script does not make much sense, but when scripts are related to one another they are discovered to fit together like parts of a jigsaw, forming a coherent whole. According to Tyrrell, 'These communicators gave clearly and candidly the reason for the cross-correspondences which they claimed to be producing. They said that they were doing it because a single theme distributed between various automatists none of whom knew what the others were writing, would prove that a single independent mind or group of minds was at the back of the whole phenomena'.[27]

Most of the allusions were to recondite and obscure points of classical literature known to the alleged respondents who were all scholars in the forefront of classical study, while the medium (Mrs Piper) and most of the automatists through whom they were working, knew no Latin or Greek and yet were writing out sentences in these languages derived from exceedingly rare and obscure authors they could never have known about. (It has been suggested that Mrs Verrall, herself a classicist and the leading automatist, was the source of the messages. But they continued after her death in 1916, and none of the other automatists had anywhere near the requisite classical background.)

One of the more simple cross-correspondences may be given as an example. In April 1907 Mrs Piper in three successive trances uttered words recorded as *Sanatos, Tanatos,* and then *Thanatos.* This final word was repeated four times. Meanwhile Mrs Fleming[28] in India wrote automatically 'Maurice, Morris, *Mors.* And with that the shadow of death fell upon him and his soul departed out of his limbs'. Mrs Verrall wrote automatically, 'Warmed both hands before the fire of life. it fails and I am ready to depart . . . Come away come away . . . *Pallida mors aequo pede pauperum tabernas regumque turres [pulsat]*'.[29]

'Thanatos', written by Mrs Piper who knew no Greek, is the Greek for 'death'; 'mors' written by Mrs Fleming who knew no Latin, is the Latin for 'death'; and of the quotations cited by Mrs Verrall, 'Come away, come away *death*' is part of a song by Shakespeare, and the Latin sentence means 'Pale death with equal foot strikes the huts of the poor and the towers of the rich'. When the three scripts arrived at the SPR it became apparent that a single theme united the three messages received from Myers by the three different people, two of whom could not have understood what they wrote.

Most of the scripts are vastly more complex and require not only a profound knowledge of the classics but also an ability to solve crossword puzzles and to spot allusions and quotations. The obscurity of the messages is part of the scheme. After all, if a person writing automatically simple wrote, 'this is from Myers, please tell everyone I have survived' the script would have no evidential value whatever. If however two uneducated people separately write half of an obscure Greek poem which after much research is tracked down to a very obscure book, and if it is later discovered that one of the alleged correspondents had lectured on this book, then the case begins to be evidential.

Thousands of scripts were received by the SPR over a thirty year period and the Second Earl Balfour and Mr J. E. Piddington devoted most of their lives to working out the correspondences between them.[30] Almost all who have made a detailed study of the scripts find them convincing.

However, the fact that the correspondences need 'working out' raises the possibility that the source of the interconnections between the scripts is the ingenuity of the living collator, rather than the mind of the departed respondent. The complexity, the allusive character and the sheer number of scripts raise this question. On the other hand, the principal scripts are available for investigation in the *Proceedings of the Society for Psychical Research*. Those who have studied them most clearly believe with W. H. Salter that 'the scheme is really there, and not an invention of the perfervid ingenuity of the interpreters, for it rests on careful documentation, painstaking research into facts, and commonsense handling of symbols and allusions'.[31] Moreover, those who actually knew the deceased, argue that the scripts are powerfully suggestive of the specific person whom they used to know. In some of the scripts they see the stamp of the alleged author's individuality all over them. For example, concerning one of Dr Verrall's scripts, his 'oldest and dearest friend', the Rev. M. A. Bayfield wrote, 'All this is Verrall's manner to the life in animated conversation . . . when I first read the words . . . I received a series of little shocks, for the turns of speech are Verrall's . . . I could hear the very tones in which he would have spoken each sentence'.[32]

Professor Gardner Murphy writes, 'The initiative seems to come from the deceased . . . there seems to be a will to communicate . . . the autonomy, the purposiveness, the cogency and above all the individuality, of the source of the messages cannot be bypassed. This looks like communion with the deceased . . .' for the 'messages were completely characteristic of themselves and of no others'.[33] For Gardner Murphy, the cross-correspondences pose an insuperable problem. Committed as he himself is to the view that 'the theoretical objections' to life after death 'are so enormous that no empirical evidence could stand against them', yet he affirms belief that the cross-correspondences do actually supply solid empirical evidence for this impossibility! There seems to him to be no way around this impasse.[34] From such a quarter, this is no insubstantial endorsement of the quality of this material. And one is tempted to wonder whether Myers in death did indeed succeed in providing what Myers in life had been searching for – evidence for the human personality's survival of bodily death. I shall return to this question in the final chapter.

7 Claimed Memories of Former Lives

Claimed memories of former lives seem to fall into two main categories. The first consists of spontaneous claims to 'remember' a past life, made by the subject while awake and fully conscious. The second consists of apparent memories which emerge in dreams, or which are articulated in response to questions asked under hypnosis when a subject has been told to 'go back in time'.[1] Let us begin by looking at alleged cases of spontaneous waking memories of former lives.

There is clearly one name which stands above all others in this field of research: that of Ian Stevenson, whose university department has systematically investigated 1300 or so cases over two decades.[2] Professor Stevenson is especially noted for his caution in an area where accusations of fraud (whether conscious or unconscious, on the part of either experimenter or subjects) are so easily made.[3] Moreover, his attention to detail and the mass of evidence he accumulates so painstakingly and meticulously place his work on quite a distinct level. Consider the following which is a précis of one case from the study he published in 1966.[4]

At the age of $4\frac{1}{2}$, a boy named Prakesh began to declare that his 'real' name was Nirmal, and that his 'real' home was in Kosi Kalan. He named 'his' father and sister, and talked of 'his father's' shops in detail and longing, and the names of many neighbours. He insisted that he be called Nirmal, and night after night he tried to run off towards Kosi Kalan, 'home'. He went on and on until his parents beat him to stop his chatter. However, unknown to his parents, Prakesh's alleged memories exactly corresponded to the life situation of a boy named Nirmal who had died shortly before Prakesh's birth. This was not discovered until five years later when Nirmal's father happened to visit Prakesh's village. Prakesh immediately recognised 'his' father and begged to be taken 'home'. This meeting led to further 'reunions' and an eventual visit to Nirmal's former home. Prakesh recognised by name and with suitable emotional overtones all Nirmal's brothers, sisters, relatives and friends. He showed intimate knowledge of the house and all its fittings, save that his knowledge was geared to the situation of ten years previous so that he was puzzled by features that had been altered in the intervening decade. Stevenson came across this case three weeks after the first 'reunion', and has set out in tabulated form 34 of Prakesh's claimed memories, the names of those who remembered him making each claimed memory prior to the 'reunion', and the names of those in the other family who could verify the accuracy of each alleged memory as a fact pertaining to the actual life-situation of Nirmal. Moreover, every member of each family testified that before the 'reunion', they had had no knowledge whatsoever of each other's families.[5]

The case is typical of those described by Stevenson in his books, except that Prakesh's exclusive identification of himself with his 'former life' is unusual. Most children in such cases would say, 'Now I'm called John, but I used to be called Fred when I was big, rather than saying, "I'm Fred, don't call me John"'.[6] But with this difference of emphasis, all the reported cases follow the same pattern. The case of a girl named Gnanatilleka is interesting, because her 'reunion' with her alleged former family was arranged by an investigating committee under strict conditions.[7] Likewise the case of a girl named Swarnlata is interesting, in that her 'former' family and home were traced for her by the parapsychology department at the University of Rajasthan on the basis of the description she gave them.[8] But the most impressive in this respect is the case of a Lebanese boy called Imad, for in this case, Stevenson arrived before anyone had tried to verify any of his alleged memories, and Stevenson was able to take down details of 47 supposed memories in writing before anyone had tried to find out to whose life-situation they might belong.[9] Further, the guesses made by Imad's parents about the possible identity of the former life were shown to be wrong,[10] so it is clear that there was no previous interaction between the two families. In spite of this, 44 out of the recorded 47 memories were found to be exactly right.[11] Moreover, as they journeyed to the home Imad claimed to remember, more memories came back to him, of which 7 included accurate knowledge about his supposed former self.[12]

Stevenson comments that far more important than the number of accurate memories is the fact that in all these cases the children's behaviour accords with the personalities of their supposed former selves. X not only claims to be Y in a new body, he also personates Y – he behaves as if he were Y being reunited to his old family. He weeps with joy to see his relatives again, he is upset and profoundly disturbed to hear of bad news affecting them; he is happier with those relatives to whom Y was particularly close than with others. His character, aptitudes, fears and pleasures are those of the person with whom he identifies. Stevenson writes, 'The identification by these children with the previous personality seems to me one of the most important features of these cases. Such personation, with components of strongly emotional behaviour, transcends the simple recital by the child of information about another person who had lived before'.[13]

Stevenson sums up the behavioural aspects of these cases thus:

'(a) Repeated statements by the subject of the identification;
(b) repeated presentation of information about the previous personality as coming to the subject in the form of memories of events experienced or of people already known;
(c) requests to go to the previous home either for a visit or permanently;
(d) familiar address and behaviour towards adults and children related to the previous personality according to the relationships and social customs which would be proper if the child really had had the relationships he claims to have had with these persons;
(e) emotional responses, e.g. of tears, joy, affection, fear or resentment appropriate for the relationships and attitudes shown by the previous personality toward other persons and objects; and
(f) mannerisms, habits, and skills which would be appropriate for the previous personality or which he was known to possess'.[14]

One final interesting feature of these studies concerns the 'fading' of general interest on the part of the subject in his former life, in his memories of it, and even of the distinctive behavioural traits (as in (f) above). For example in the case of Sunil Dutt Saxena who claimed to remember being a wealthy business man, Seth Sri Krishna, Stevenson reports: 'In 1971 Sunil (who was then 12 years old) has almost completely forgotten about the previous life and had entirely lost the features of his behaviour which had set him apart from his siblings and which corresponded closely to similar traits reported for Seth Sri Krishna'.[15] Although this is commonly the pattern, it is not invariably followed, and there are cases in which memories and some characteristic behavioural traits may linger on.[16]

Now whatever other interpretation we may choose to give to the data Stevenson has collected, one option seems not to be open. Fraud, whether intentional or unintentional, by Stevenson himself, his co-workers, or the subjects of their studies and their families and other witnesses, is not a plausible 'explanation'. The sheer thoroughness of Stevenson's methods precludes it for the cases he himself is prepared to endorse. Every witness was subjected to rigorous questioning, careful notes were taken of what was said and these were checked against a second inquiry some years later. Further, in some of these cases, Stevenson was able to compare his information with that acquired by other serious investigators.[17] The sheer numbers of witnesses involved would also make a conspiracy of fraud difficult, especially when sustained for several years. Further to these considerations we must add the difficulty of directing and staging the highly emotional scenes Stevenson observed. And in the case of Imad the hypothesis of fraud seems particularly to be ruled out by the fact that Stevenson conducted the full inquiry himself and learned that the preliminary hypothesis of Imad's parents was wholly false, and that therefore they could not have organised a fraud.

The only hypothesis which might enable one to discount the evidence is that of casting doubt on Stevenson's intellectual integrity. Unfortunately, some writers in this field are not always above twisting the data to fit their beliefs.[18] But it is just not plausible to write Stevenson off as being so keen to convince us of the truth of reincarnation that he misrepresents matters to fit his case. For he lists all the 'wrong' memories as well as those which turned out to be correct; and he does not try to make weak cases appear stronger than the evidence warrants. Moreover, he gives careful consideration to various possible hypotheses (including cryptomnesia, i.e. the submerged memory of events forgotten by the conscious self) to account for the data, and even though he concludes that reincarnation is the most plausible, this is for him a bone fide conclusion and not a preconceived result he has set out to prove.

I shall take up this question of how such data are to be interpreted later. First, let us move on to review cases where the alleged memories only emerge in dreams, or when under hypnosis a person is asked to 'remember' events of a previous life. Perhaps the best known case here is that of 'Ruth Mill Simmons',[19] who under hypnosis apparently recalled vividly and accurately a previous life in nineteenth-century Ireland as Bridey Murphy. However, this case illustrates rather clearly the difficulty of establishing the evidential character of such information. For it has been claimed that subsequent research suggests that Ruth Simmons was recalling not 'her own' memories of a former life, but rather she was bringing into consciousness and dramatising as her own experience, vivid stories about life in Ireland told to her in childhood by acquaintances of Irish extraction.

Yet there are cases of claimed memories that emerge under hypnosis or in dreams which do not seem so easily squeezed into this 'reductive' explanatory mould. First there are cases which seem to supply accurate historical information transcending anything which might be considered readily available to non-experts. Secondly, and even more puzzling, are reported cases of responsive xenoglossy, i.e. where the subject under hypnosis is said to be able to converse in a language unknown to him otherwise, and which he seems not to have learned by any normal means.

Some of the most well-publicised cases in recent years of detailed historical memories belong to the Bloxham tape collection as researched by Jeffrey Iverson.[20] Of particular interest is the subject 'Jane Evans'[21] who was regressed to seven quite different lives. Three of these lives particularly lend themselves to historical investigation. In these, Mrs Evans appears to relive, in the role of a minor character, situations whose features can be checked against documented historical facts. On the 'plus' side for the reincarnationist there are four major considerations. First while under hypnosis subjects often identify completely with the person whose life they seem to be remembering. Indeed, they may show signs of suffering if they report 'reliving' some nasty experience.[22] Moreover some stories, and in particular those of Mrs Evans, are not only detailed; they are also, by and large, consistent with what is known of the history of the relevant period. Thirdly, the perspectives from which the subjects tell their stories are in keeping with the characters they personate. For example, Mrs Evans often shows no knowledge of some of the best-known text-book facts about the situations she describes, where such facts would not have been available to the ordinary eye-witness who really was 'there' at the time, and whose view of events would inevitably have been limited. Now if the subject has in fact read or heard stories about the events she relates, but has forgotten them in her conscious mind, it is surprising that she seems not to know some of the most commonly cited historical details. What is so hard to understand is the apparent selection and arrangement of the material. Certainly, it would seem to be an extremely complicated process to sift through the data, extracting precisely that which is commensurate with the life-situation of a relatively insignificant individual while dispensing totally with the rest. Fourthly, it has been claimed, at least for Jane Evans, that she supplies historical details which were unknown to experts of the relevant period, but which were subsequently verified.[23]

But there are also many points on the 'minus' side. First, we cannot take the indubitable reality of the experience for the subject as he 'relives' some often extremely unpleasant experiences while under hypnosis or in dreams, to indicate anything more than that the subject is not pretending. Even if physical symptoms of disease, injury or extreme pain are manifested, this does not in itself suffice to show that the subject really once was the person with whom he identifies. As Stevenson has pointed out, mystics have also developed physical signs such as stigmata, by intense identification with the crucified Christ.[24] But we do not conclude that these individuals are reincarnations of Jesus.

Secondly, not all of the details given by the subjects are considered by experts to be right for an eye-witness in the situation as described.[25] Moreover, it strikes one immediately how much Mrs Evans' (who is Bloxham's 'best' case) most impressive lives read like historical romances. So often, near-historical novels weave a plausible tale around some lesser (or even fictional) character through whose eyes we see a major historical drama unfold. Further the author of such a work may use it to air some pet theory on a subject for which the historical details are tantalisingly missing. Now Mrs Evans seems in many of her 'lives' to re-enact the role of a minor figure in the history of some notable person or event. And in one case in particular, she 'fills in' some highly plausible details about the lives of some of the best-known personalities in the Roman world.[26] Now I am not suggesting that what Mrs Evans is doing is a straightforward rehearsal of some elements in an historical novel which she has long-since consciously forgotten. But it does not seem entirely implausible that some combination of cryptomnesia involving the use of such material plus dramatisation might account for her 'memories'.

There is one final enormous difficulty with taking these reports at their face value as evidential of genuine personal memories, namely that of language. Iverson does not feel that the failure of subjects like Jane Evans to speak the natural languages of their other personnae is necessarily a threat to their testimony. He writes: 'No one is certain what areas [of the brain] are being activated under hypnosis. Memories, in any case, are frequently divorced from speech . . . One of Bloxham's subjects told me being regressed was a mainly visual experience supplemented by "words which just pop into your head" '.[27] He suggests that hypnotic regression may involve something similar to electrode stimulation of the brain during which patients vividly recall former experiences which they see, as if it were a film-strip running in their heads.[28] But even with these pleas in mitigation, the problem remains. For it is no longer acceptable to think of language as just a means of naming private experiences. Rather, in the light of twentieth-century philosophy we have come to realise that what we see and experience is intimately linked with the language we use to report such experiences, whether to others or even to ourselves. It is thus highly implausible that so central a feature of someone's mental life as the language he spoke and in which he formulated his thoughts, should disappear completely in his 'reincarnation'.[29] In short, the absence of ability to speak the appropriate language counts strongly against any claim that the subject really once was the person whose life he or she seems to remember.

However, there have been some reported cases of responsive xenoglossy in which the subject under hypnosis was apparently able to converse in the language of the individual whose life he or she seemed to remember.[30] For example, Stevenson has mentioned the following two cases. One subject 'assumed the personality of a Norseman of mediaeval times and conversed in the dialect [of early Norwegian] although still capable of understanding some English'.[31] Another case involved an American woman, Lydia Johnson, who in earlier sessions of hypnosis spoke broken English punctuated with foreign words, but later spoke almost entirely in Swedish. She 'became' a seventeenth-century Swedish farmer called Jansen Jacoby. But experiments were hastily wound up when Jacoby 'reappeared' unbidden and without the prior hypnosis of the subject.[32] Similarly, Leslie Weatherhead cites the case of a Lancashire woman, Annie Baker, who, it was alleged, was able under hypnosis (though not otherwise) to speak fluent French.[33] This lady apparently gave details of a former life during the French Revolution.

So what are we to make of these strange tales? The 'normal' explanation, namely cryptomnesia, is supported by at least three psychological considerations. First, under hypnosis people are usually extremely suggestible and anxious to oblige; secondly hypnosis can enable them to recall long-forgotten information and past experiences; and thirdly, almost all of us have, according to Anthony Storr, a 'B-movie' permanently running in our subconscious.[34] However, at first sight the cryptomnesia hypothesis might appear intrinsically implausible for cases where the subjects seem to supply impressively detailed information about history. For example, on reading the summary given in the secondary literature of a woman who 'remembered' in dreams life during the Cathar persecution of the thirteenth century, one might well feel that here was a cast iron case of inexplicable historical knowledge.[35]

Turning to the original source material, however, it becomes apparent that the woman who possessed these 'memories' had a singular capacity for unconscious memorising. For example, as a school girl, she had almost been expelled for cheating on the grounds that an examination script contained verbatim extracts from a commentary on poetry. She saved herself from the ignominy by reproducing under closer supervision the same passages.[36] Likewise in later life she burnt a novel she had written after she discovered that much of it was verbally very similar to an article which she could not recall having read. But having stumbled on this article, she called her own work 'unconscious plagiarism'.[37] For these reasons she herself refused to believe in her supposed 'reincarnation' – a point insufficiently noted in the secondary literature.[38]

Moreover, concerning claimed historical memories which emerge under hypnotic regression, such as those in the Bloxham collection, there are two vexing omissions. First, it is a great pity that Bloxham seems not to have invited professional historians to supply questions whose answers might have provided a strong indication, one way or the other, as to the evidential quality of the subjects' 'memories'. Secondly, some experimenters like E. S. Zolick,[39] who have used hypnotic regression on patients, have in subsequent sessions asked the hypnotised subject what the source of his information was. Bloxham, however, does not seem to have tried this line of questioning. Now I am not suggesting that such tests could prove conclusively whether or not the knowledge hypnotised subjects seem to have is explicable by some purely 'normal' hypothesis. But it would at least narrow the possibilities. In particular, when subjects seem to know some very obscure historical facts, it would be helpful if we could be sure about two points: (a) the veracity of the subjects' statements; and (b) that the previously 'unknown' data they provide are really just that. This latter point is potentially highly significant. Much is made of subjects' apparent knowledge which is subsequently verified by 'surprised' experts.[40] The problem is to assess the significance of such claims. Often, the cases involve trivial 'facts' which might either be accidentally true (because they are not *prime facie* unlikely anyway), or they might be reasonable speculations on the part of the author of the (forgotten) source of the subject's information, or they might possibly be less 'unknown' than proponents of reincarnation claim. The re-incarnationist case would be more convincing if subjects were to supply answers to concrete questions concerning, for example, the exact whereabouts of a particular building which is known to have existed, but which has never been located in modern times.[41]

Even so, it has to be admitted that there are some puzzling aspects of cases where subjects have historically accurate, verifiable and detailed knowledge going far beyond anything found in the classic case which is usually cited as evidence for the cryptomnesia hypothesis, namely Zolick's work on 'the previous existence fantasy',[42] or in the historical literature available to the non-expert. And in the absence of adequate substantiation either way, it remains at least possible that there may be some cases of hypnotically induced or dreamed 'memories' of former lives which cannot be fully explained by the cryptomnesia hypothesis.

Moreover, responsive xenoglossy is particularly unsuited to this sort of reductive explanation. It may be that on occasion, someone unwittingly stores some foreign phrases in his unconscious memory, and that these phrases can be retrieved under hypnosis.[43] But it is less plausible to think that on the basis of, say, gazing absent-mindedly at an old Swedish volume or perhaps seeing a film, a subject might glean enough information to infer correctly the rules and vocabulary of seventeenth century Swedish and apply them!

Yet such is the 'explanation' which a cryptomnesia hypothesis offers in the case of Lydia Johnson/Jansen Jacoby.

In sum, then, there seem to be a wide variety of cases brought together under hypnotic regression and dream experiences. Some may be little more than wish-fulfilment fantasies or the products of lively imaginations. Sometimes, such fantasies may be woven around ideas not consciously remembered in walking life, and may even involve strong identification by the subject with the character in his fantasy. Still others may owe a great deal to suggestions implanted by the hypnotist. But when we have eliminated all these 'normal' explanations, we seem to be left with a residuum of cases which are not so readily dismissed. Of these, providing we can eliminate the possibility of fraud or misrepresentation, instances of responsive xenoglossy must come at the top of the list. But it is just possible that there are some cases of historical 'memories' which are so rich in obscure but potentially verifiable detail, that a 'normal' explanation might not do them justice. Likewise, Stevenson's accounts of claimed waking memories are not satisfactorily explicable by a cryptomnesia hypothesis. The former lives which his subjects claim to remember are usually of very ordinary folk. Thus in most cases, the only possible 'normal' source of the subjects' knowledge about the life of the deceased would be from living people. But how then could they spontaneously recognise people and places? Moreoever, when we consider the relative isolation which village life and the caste system impose on many of Stevenson's respondents, and also the lengths to which Stevenson goes to establish that the families involved knew nothing of one another prior to the child's voicing his claimed memories, the cryptomnesia hypothesis must surely be discounted.[44]

Stevenson considers that in the absence of any satisfactory 'normal' explanations for the data he has collected, we are obliged to take seriously the possibility of paranormal accounts. He reviews various possibilities like telepathy or other sorts of E.S.P. or communication with a surviving personality (or part-personality), and argues convincingly why none of these accounts does full justice to many of his cases.[45] He concludes that 'for some of the cases all the facts are better accounted for by supposing a continuing influence of the previous personality after death'.[46] Thus for Stevenson, the spontaneous waking 'memories' his subjects have point towards either reincarnation or possession, cases falling 'along a continuum in which the distinction between reincarnation and possession becomes blurred'.[47] So too with cases of responsive xenoglossy, he comments 'when we can exclude normal acquisition of knowledge of the foreign language by the subject, the explanatory hypotheses become helpfully reduced and almost restricted to possession and reincarnation'.[48]

Stevenson presents a strong case therefore, for saying that at least some claimed 'memories of a former life' appear to be evidential for and suggestive of some theory of reincarnation or possession. However, what significance such conclusions would have for belief in personal survival of bodily death, and how they might cohere with the other considerations we have discussed in earlier chapters are questions which we must now try to answer.

Part Four

Part four

8 Immortality or Extinction?

I have tried to show that whether or not there can be any personal survival of bodily death is a substantive issue which cannot be decided merely by examining the meanings of words as used in everyday situations. Further, I have argued that the central Christian message of a future hope is precisely that and not some this-world only doctrine dressed up in the imagery of the language of resurrection, immortality and eternal life. But it is one thing to show that talk of life after death which refers to some possible future beyond the grave is not meaningless, and quite another to establish that it represents any plausible outcome.

Belief in a future life is seriously threatened not only by the naturalistic case for extinction, but also by the demise of the traditional Christian doctrinal framework. Increasingly, the natural sciences are weaving a coherent and unified explanatory web for all natural phenomena. And man himself is not exempt. Rather he also seems to be but a part of the natural world. As Gardner Murphy claims, 'the intimate unity of psychological and physiological processes . . . makes the conception of an independent soul recede more and more into the land of the utterly incredible and unimaginable'.[1] Moreover, realisation of just how much a part of nature man is must force reassessment of any belief that he is somehow different in kind from everything else in the universe. For the absence of sharp cut-off lines, whether in the development of the individual or of the species, makes it impossible on the basis of any objective and non-arbitrary criteria, to distinguish a group of potentially immortal creatures which are manifestly different from all other types. Nor can we get around this problem by arguing that man is not the only creature who will be preserved. For wherever we might try to draw a dividing line there would be some element of arbitrariness involved. And I find it impossible to make any sort of sense, naturalistic or religious, of the idea that everything will be saved.

So in the face of such seemingly overwhelming arguments, we

must ask ourselves whether the religious believer can rationally maintain that man survives bodily death. For to take the evidence of the natural sciences seriously is to recognise a bitter-sweet irony. The very scientific knowledge which has enabled man to rise above nature seems, in another sense, to show that he belongs there and nowhere else.

But what if everything does not 'fit'? What if there should be 'facts' which cannot be accommodated within this impressive edifice? One's first intuitive response is to write off any such claims – everything must ultimately fit because that is the way reality is. At least the intellectual air we breathe reinforces such an assumption at almost every turn. Any alleged 'facts' which appear to threaten this current orthodoxy are more likely than not to be ignored if not positively ridiculed. For whether or not any particular belief is deemed reasonable depends on two factors: first the evidence for it and secondly its coherence within the overall world-view of the person forming the assessment, even though that view may not itself be entirely internally consistent. Thus very little evidence is required for us to accept as true an alleged fact which fits easily enough into the framework of the rest of our thought. But if we are asked to give credence to something fundamentally at variance with our other convictions about the nature of reality, we will require a quality of evidence of a wholly different order before we take it seriously. As C. D. Broad comments in connection with the evidence for paranormal claims, 'It is certainly right to demand a much higher standard of evidence for events which are alleged to be paranormal than those which would be normal . . . For in dealing with evidence we have always to take into account the antecedent probability or improbability of the alleged event, i.e. its probability or improbability relative to all the rest of our knowledge and well-founded belief other than the special evidence adduced in its favour'.[2]

Some would go further than this and say that no evidence could ever suffice to establish as true something which contradicted their total world-view. For example, the nineteenth century scientist, Hermann von Helmholtz, rejected telepathy as quite impossible and declared that 'neither the testimony of all the Fellows of the Royal Society nor the evidence of my own senses, would lead me to believe in the transmission of thoughts from one person to another independently of the recognised channels of sense'.[3] And as we noted in chapter 1, it was this sort of thinking which brought about the confrontation of the Church with Galileo. If one is convinced that one 'knows' the nature of reality, all appeals to evidence become superfluous.

Happily dogmatism of this type is becoming increasingly rare, both in the fields of religion and science. Moreover, it is now generally accepted that major advances in science almost always involve some fundamental rethinking so that a belief which was once held to be beyond question may be overthrown. At very least, it may be necessary to hold disparate beliefs in tension while waiting for further clarification. As the anthropologist, Margaret Mead reminded the American Association for the Advancement of Science in her speech advocating the admission of the Parapsychological Association to that body, 'The whole history of scientific advance is full of scientists investigating phenomena that the Establishment did not believe were there'.[4] Need we then be so concerned about the anomalous nature of psi-phenomena relative to our present scientific theories?

Unfortunately, the implied analogy between past scientific revolutions and present acceptance of parapsychology is by no means exact. To illustrate the differences, let us look briefly at one scientific revolution which was particularly 'shocking' because it overthrew our fundamental assumptions about causality.

One of the basic premises underlying almost all scientific explanation is that everything that happens should be explicable in terms of antecedent causal factors. Or to put it another way, we assume that things just do not happen without a cause. Yet the quantum theory undermines this fundamental assumption at the level of sub-micro events. The problem is not just that particle physicists have as yet failed to find any causal explanation for randomness at the sub-micro level. Rather, it turns out to be an essential element in the theory itself that individual events must be indeterminate.[5] Yet once we move out of the world of particle physics and into the more familiar realm of medium-sized objects, our 'old' ideas about causality work well enough. And there is no contradiction. The magnitude of the indeterminacy is so small that it can be detected only on the sub-atomic scale; and moreover where vast numbers of sub-atomic particles are involved (as they are in any object we can actually see) the statistical averaging out of individual uncertainties gives a result which is essentially equivalent to the old notion of causal determination. In short, even though the scientific revolution has shown us that causality is not a fundamental principle applicable to everything that happens, yet it is a satisfactory working principle when we are dealing with phenomena above the level of sub-micro events. There is no suggestion of some ineffable inexplicability about the phenomena we observe in the world. For even the 'indeterminate' behaviour of fundamental particles is encompassed by the basic relations which obtain at that level.

Nowhere in the history of scientific revolutions have we been obliged to accept that there appears, *ex nihilo*, something fundamentally inexplicable whose behaviour is said to lack any material basis. Yet this is precisely what we are being asked to swallow with the psi-hypothesis. For its basic claim is that conscious creatures are able to perform feats (like telepathy or observing from outside the body) which rest on no underlying physico-chemical mechanisms.

Now clearly, every scientific theory which has ever been put forward has left some loose ends untied. And in general, such 'niggling problems' tend not to be seen as posing any serious threat to a theory which has proved its worth through its general applicability, its systematising power and its predictive and explanatory successes. Rather they are set aside as minor inconsistencies which will probably be sorted out later. The problems come if they remain obdurately and intractably anomalous. For then doubts begin insidiously to creep in that perhaps the beautiful systematic theory is not quite perfect after all. And if someone comes up with a new theory which can encompass these oddities as well as making just as good sense otherwise as the old theory did, then it is likely to be accepted – albeit with some rearguard action from the established orthodoxy – as a replacement for the old theory.[6] Now psi-data stick out like very sore thumbs from the theories of the natural sciences. And our problem is that we cannot at present see how any replacement theory could satisfactorily encompass both the normal and the paranormal data, integrating them into a systematic and unified whole. Rather we seem to be faced with two sorts of data, pointing towards apparently irreconcilable inferences. As Gardner Murphy commented in exasperation: 'What happens when an irresistible force meets an immovable object? To me the evidence cannot be by-passed, nor, on the other hand, can conviction be achieved'.[7]

But what conclusions follow from accepting the validity of such evidence as cannot be by-passed? It might perhaps be thought from the order in which the paranormal data were presented in chapters

5, 6 and 7, that we suppose that near-death experiences open up the door to survival, cross-correspondences show that such survival is not ephemeral, and reincarnation follows to enable the personality to go on to further development and growth in other lives. Such a schema seems to enjoy a fair measure of support even among Christians today, inasmuch as virtually as many Anglicans believe in reincarnation as believe in heaven and hell.[8] But I suggest that as a theory of personal survival of death, such a scheme is not intelligible. The evidence for reincarnation points not to immortality but to extinction. To show that this is so, let us suppose that at least some of the data supplied by Ian Stevenson and Arnall Bloxham provide sufficient grounds for belief in either 'reincarnation' or 'possession'; and let us see what implications follow from these two hypotheses.

Interpreting the data as evidence for reincarnation, we would say that many children, particularly in the East, have some memories of an earlier existence and have some behavioural traits in common with that former life. In a few cases these memories are fairly extensive, but will tend to fade as the child grows up unless reinforced by constant recollection. However, the vast majority of mankind has no conscious memories of any previous existence. On the other hand, unconscious memories of such lives occasionally come out in dreams, and under hypnosis almost all of us will vividly recall our previous existences. Such is the picture we get if we take the reincarnation interpretation of the evidence from claimed memories of former lives at its face value. But does it add up to life after death?

I suggest that each reader ask himself that question with direct relation to his own future destiny. Let me answer this inquiry as it relates to me. Suppose that for a few years after my death a child between the ages of three and ten claims to recall a number of accurate memories of my life, manifests some of my distinctive behavioural traits and identifies himself with me. Would 'I' really live again during that seven year period, given that as a happily married university lecturer my central sense of identity arises out of my work of academic research and teaching and in my marital relationship, neither of which could be internally intelligible to any child? Since his 'memories' would probably fade before he reached the age when abstract conceptual thought or a mature personal relationship were possible for him, it is hard to see how my present self-hood could be continuous with his. Likewise, let us suppose that hundreds of years hence some person belonging to a wholly alien culture were to visit a hypnotist and for an hour or so 'remember' and personate some critical episode in my present life. This is all that the evidence adds up to. It is hard to see how it can begin to be regarded as ensuring my personal survival of bodily death.

What about the possession hypothesis? For this we must assume that after my death some memories of my present existence with a few of my behavioural traits will cluster together to form something akin to what C. D. Broad calls a 'psychic factor'.[9] For most of us this psychic factor will exist in a kind of limbo, but in a few cases it will succeed briefly in entering into and influencing the developing mind of some young child, or perhaps after a few centuries it will have one glorious hour of self-expression through the hypnotised body of some future person.

I do not pretend to be able to give a more satisfactory explanation for the baffling phenomenon of persons apparently correctly 'remembering' former lives, than the reincarnation or possession hypotheses discussed by Ian Stevenson. But it needs to be remembered that eliminating all the other explanatory hypotheses which have been put forward does not compel one to embrace whatever happens to be left. We might conclude that the phenomenon was simply inexplicable at our present state of knowledge, and wait further inspiration! However, my present purpose is not to offer any explanation for these claimed memories but only to point out that neither reincarnation nor possession could ensure my survival. Moreover, I would like to endorse John Hick's judgement that the persistence of some isolated cluster of my memories and dispositions would be 'equally compatible with the extinction of the personality as a whole or with its continued life in some other sphere'.[10] Hence on such a view, claimed memories of former lives are irrelevant to the central question of personal immortality or extinction.

The same cannot be said of the other paranormal data we have discussed. Near-death experiences are highly relevant to the question of survival for they seem to point, if only for a moment at the brink of death, to a real separation between the self and its normal embodiment. And although it is true that near-death experiences on their own could be compatible with supposing that shortly after bodily death the self also perishes, they are equally compatible with the belief that the self continues in being. The supreme barrier against belief in a future life is the doctrine that mind and body are inseparably united. If even one out-of-the-body experience is correctly described as such this barrier crumbles and life after death becomes an open possibility.

This possibility would become more solid if it could be established that a veridical communication had been received from a deceased person. Many who believe that they have seen an apparition of a deceased relative or friend find this experience personally convincing.[11] And of course for Christians, the historical foundation of their future hope is the belief that Jesus *'appeared'* to many of his disciples after his death,[12] 'to whom he shewed himself alive . . . by many infallible proofs, being seen of them forty days'.[13] For those seeking 'stricter' evidence, the best to be found seems to be that of the cross-correspondence cases which we discussed in chapter 6. Even these cannot provide indisputable proof of personal survival, but they are remarkably suggestive.

But to what kind of next world does such evidence point? Near-death experiences would seem to suggest a future life in which we would be but mute and invisible spectators, trapped in a world of memories and observations. Now we might try to circumvent this rather unattractive conclusion by supposing that such a state represented only an intermediate stage between this life and the next. After all, everyone who has survived to tell of his or her near-death experience has been 'dragged back' and did not move on to the supposed new life. However it is striking that the alleged authors of the cross-correspondence cases do not seem to have 'moved on'. Although as Broad says, 'the best of the cross-correspondence cases . . . seem to suggest the persistence of something which forms plans after death and takes measures to fulfil them',[14] yet all these plans centre on a goal originally formulated while on earth, namely proving survival. As Hick observes, they 'say nothing about the nature of their present existence, and give no impression of living a real life, in another environment'.[15]

Tyrrell seeks to account for the problem by suggesting that telepathic communication between such different modes of being might be very difficult.[16] We might also make the point that none of the books which Myers, for example, wrote during his earthly life said anything about the nature of his then existence and gave no impression of any wider interests than passionate concern about the survival problem. It would be completely in keeping if such oblivion to mundane details of everyday life continued to characterise his attitude in the hereafter! Nevertheless, it remains surprising that of the thousands of messages allegedly sent over a thirty year period, none gives any hint of new interests developed in the next life.

But perhaps a next life which was a mind-dependent world,[17] based upon experiences and memories from this one, might not be as negative a prospect as this discussion supposes. When deprived of any further sensory stimuli from our now defunct sense organs, our minds might think into existence a world of mental images somewhat akin to the dreams we now have, but more under our conscious control. Such a post-mortem world would be shaped by our characters as formed during earthly life. One consequence of such a notion is that through reliving our memories and exploring in imagination our desires we might come to re-evaluate the thoughts and actions of our earthly life, and an element of self-judgement would arise in the light of such reflections. Nor need our mind-dependent world be wholly solipsistic; for with the supply of sensory data cut off, telepathy with others might well come into its own as a vivid channel of communication and dialogue.

However it could be argued that a mind-dependent world does not provide a satisfactory environment for a truly personal life after death. A world of mental images is essentially a world of memory, thought and contemplation, not one of challenge and responsibility. Could it therefore fulfil the aims envisaged for it? Reflections can indeed provide the spark for reform, but should not action follow if reformation is really to be achieved? Likewise, although telepathy could provide rapport with other minds, it would seem that almost all such communication would inevitably be related to past experiences unless future activity were open to the agents concerned. Even the best of old comrades would ultimately tire of exchanging memories of the past or weaving new theories about what might have been. And with no fresh input, a mind-dependent world might eventually come to seem futile and empty. Indeed Sir Peter Strawson suggests that 'as memories fade and this vicarious living palls' the individual's concept of himself would become attenuated; and 'at the limit of attenuation' there would be 'from the point of view of his survival as an individual, no difference between the continuance of experience and its cessation'.[18]

Now we must surely concur with Strawson's assessment as long as we ignore the religious dimension. On an atheistic presumption, near-death experiences might encourage belief in a temporary survival for human personality, but they could not guarantee an eternal destiny. However, from a religious view-point, any atheistic evaluation of a mind-dependent world leaves out one crucial factor – knowledge of God. If it is possible for man to enter into a direct relationship with God, such an encounter could not be mediated through the senses, but rather must come through some process akin to telepathy. Claimed religious experience is far more common in this life than is claimed telepathic rapport with other human minds. In a mind-dependent world where telepathy and religious experience would come into their own, we would expect religious experience to retain its relative dominance, and God to become the most vital subject of our experiencing. The witness of the mystics of all religious traditions is that the practice of mental prayer in the life of contemplation greatly enhances the sense of communion with God. Such conditions could be particularly well realised in a mind-dependent world. Likewise all the saints have urged that the beatific vision could never cloy or cease to be utterly fulfilling and absorbing.[19] Thus St Thomas Aquinas asserts, 'Nothing that is contemplated with wonder can be tiresome, since as long as the thing remains in wonder it continues to stimulate desire. But the divine substance is always viewed with wonder by any created intellect . . . so it is impossible for an intellectual substance to become tired of this vision'.[20] This may sound dry in Aquinas' formal language, but the same sentiment is expressed with rather more emotional content by many Christian believers who claim with Augustine that the human heart can find no true rest till it rests on God's eternal changelessness.[21] This aspect of the beatific vision needs to be stressed. For eternity is not simply endless duration, but a state in which time ceases to have relevance or meaning. Since we would expect a disembodied existence to be outside time as well as outside matter, this emphasis would seem entirely appropriate.

However, such a world would be a satisfying permanent future only for a person with a developed mind and mystical religious sensitivity. An infant would lack the mental resources for such a world, and adults with an entirely secular outlook or with religious sentiments confined to the political versions of their creeds would not be themselves if they found such a life congenial.[22]

For these sorts of reasons, John Hick suggests that for most people a mind-dependent world would be only a temporary stage for reflection before the self would move on to re-embodiment in a new kind of life. This thought corresponds to the notion deeply rooted in traditional Christianity that the persistence of the soul in a disembodied state is unnatural to it, and that eventually the soul must be 'clothed upon' by a new body if the person is truly to live again. Moreover, although popular Hinduism and Buddhism teach a this-worldly interpretation of reincarnation, there are many references in their scriptures to re-birth normally taking place in other worlds.[23] Given this understanding of the eastern tradition, one can seek Hick's proposal as providing a global approach to the theology of death. It attempts to draw the major speculations about our possible destiny from the philosophical and religious writings of both east and west into a coherent and unified hypothesis. For it equates both resurrection and reincarnation with the notion of the conscious personal self surviving bodily death and subsequently receiving a new embodiment for life in another space. Many believe that the notion of plural spaces, on which this hypothesis depends, is perfectly thinkable. Indeed, according to Karl Heim, if we take modern physics seriously we must 'from the outset be prepared to accept the possibility of beings which live in a space pattern that is completely inaccessible to us'.[24] If this is so, there would appear to be no problem about the location of a spatial resurrection world which forms no part of this universe and is in no spatio-temporal relationship with it.[25] It might even seem possible to embrace with John Hick the notion of a whole succession of other worlds in which we would live a variety of further lives with intervals for reflection in mind-dependent existences, before we eventually develop to the final state of the beatific vision.[26]

But it must be stressed that the future hope as thus outlined, though conceivable, runs flat against the well-founded assumptions of the naturalistic world-view which has been built up in recent centuries. It also extends substantially beyond the slight bridge-head established by a particular interpretation of some paranormal phenomena whose authenticity is not universally accepted. On what, then, does this hope rely? We have seen in chapter 4 that it can no longer be securely based on the integrated framework of traditional Christian doctrine. On the other hand, ever since Schleiermacher's *Speeches on Religion* of 1799, modern theology has laid its stress not on the doctrinal formulations of its historic creeds, but on the living experience of God, both within the Christian community and in the wider religious experience of the human race. One central element of this experience is the sense of entering a living relationship with God and trusting in the reality of that fellowship against the force of death.[27] Throughout history it is probable that this has been the decisive element in the case for belief in a future life. As Edward Schillebeeckx writes: 'The breeding ground of belief in life after death . . . was always seen in a communion of life between God and man . . . Living communion with God, attested as the meaning, the foundation and the inspiring content of human existence, is the only climate in which the believer's trust in a life after death comes, and evidently can come, to historical fruition'.[28]

To many this will seem an exceedingly frail foundation on which to build so momentous a claim. But for those to whom God is a reality, no basis could be more secure.

Notes and References

CHAPTER 1: The Logic of Mortality

1. A. Flew, *Body, Mind and Death* (Macmillan, 1964) p. 12.
2. A. Flew and A. MacIntyre, *New Essays in Philosophical Theology* (SCM, 1963) p. 269.
3. A. Flew, *Body, Mind and Death*, p. 4.
4. E.g. G. Ryle, *The Concept of Mind* (Penguin, 1966); P. F. Strawson, *Individuals* (Methuen, 1965); T. Penelhum, *Survival and Disembodied Existence* (RKP, 1970).
5. A. Flew, *A Dictionary of Philosophy* (Pan, 1979) p. 348.
6. L. Wittgenstein, *Tractatus Logico-Philosophicus* 6.431 and 6.1411, cited in Flew and MacIntyre, *New Essays*, p. 272.
7. The title of an article by Dr E. Kubler Ross published in *Co-evolution Quarterly*, (Summer 1977).
8. J. Macquarrie, *Principles of Christian Theology* (SCM, 1966) p. 69.
9. R. Lawler, D. W. Wuerl and T. C. Lawler, *The Teaching of Christ: a Catholic Catechism for Adults* (Veritas, 1976) p. 544. This Catechism was published with the commendation of Cardinal Conway, Primate of all Ireland, and of Archbishop Bernadin, President of the United States National Conference of Catholic Bishops, as a clear presentation of what the Catholic Church teaches.
10. Augustine, *City of God*, Bk. 22, ch. 20.
11. Rufinus, *The Apostles' Creed*, para. 43.
12. P. Badham, *Christian Beliefs about Life after Death* (Macmillan, 1976) pp. 79ff.
13. J. Macquarrie, *The Christian Hope* (Mowbrays, 1978) p. 117.
14. Cf. B. Williams, *Problems of the Self* (CUP, 1973) chapter 5.
15. Flew and MacIntyre, *New Essays*, p. 268.
16. A. Flew in J. R. Smythies, *Brain and Mind* (RKP, 1965) p. 25.
17. A. J. Ayer, *The Central Questions of Philosophy* (Penguin, 1976) p. 133.
18. Cf. T. Kuhn, *The Structure of Scientific Revolutions* (Univ. of Chicago, 1970); P. Feyerabend, 'Explanation, Reduction and Empiricism', in H. Feigl and G. Maxwell, (eds) *Minnesota Studies in the Philosophy of Science* vol. iii (Univ. of Minnesota, 1962); M. Hesse, 'Is there an Independent Observation Language?', in N. Colodny, *The Nature and Function of Scientific Theories* (Univ. of Pittsburg, 1970) pp. 275–353; and R. Harré and E. H. Madden, *Causal Powers* (Blackwell, 1975) pp. 21ff.
19. Flew and MacIntyre, *New Essays*, p. 269; and A. Flew, *The Presumption of Atheism* (Elek, 1976) p. 128.
20. Cf. Ayer, *The Central Questions*, p. 133.

21. I am constantly feeling left out of such discussions as I have tried in vain to see after images of any kind!
22. Williams, *Problems of the Self* pp. 42–5.
23. Flew, *Presumption*, p. 110.
24. Cf. D. M. Armstrong, *A Materialist Theory of Mind* (RKP, 1968) p. 74.
25. Flew, *Body, Mind and Death*, p. 10.
26. For defence of this see H. D. Lewis, *The Elusive Mind* (Allen and Unwin, 1969) and Part 2 of my own *Christian Beliefs*
27. Cf. W. Kneale, *On Having a Mind* (CUP, 1962) pp. 50–2.
28. Williams, *Problems of the Self*, p. 14.
29. Cf. Badham, *Christian Beliefs*, pp. 100ff. for a fuller discussion.
30. Williams, *Problems of the Self*, pp. 46–63.
31. A. Flew in Smythies, *Brain and Mind*, p. 27.
32. Flew, *Presumption*, p. 149.
33. The evidence for supposed mediumistic communication will be considered in chapter 6.
34. Psalm 90.9.
35. Acts 20.38.
36. Plato, *Phaedo* 59E–61B, 117A–118. In the translation by H. Tredennick, *The Last Days of Socrates* (Penguin, 1959). On p. 100 Plato denies there was any sense of sorrow at Socrates' death, but this is wholly contradicted by the evidence he later cites, not only of Xanthippe's distress (p. 102), but of the profound distress of all Socrates' disciples (p. 182).
37. *Roman Missal in Latin and English* (Pre-Vatican 2 Version, Belgium 1961) p. 238.
38. R. H. Thouless, 'Theories about survival', *Journal of the Society for Psychical Research*, Vol. 50, no. 779 (March 1979)
39. Ayer, *The Central Questions*, p. 124.
40. Lewis Caroll, *Through the Looking Glass* (Piccolo, 1977 (1871)) chapter 6, p. 74.

CHAPTER 2 : The Meaning of Resurrection, Immortality and Eternal Life

1. G. Kaufman, *Systematic Theology* (Scribner, 1968) p. 464.
2. S. Ogden, *The Reality of God* (SCM, 1967) p. 230.
3. Cf. Chapter 2 of Paul Badham, *Christian Beliefs about Life after Death* (Macmillan, 1976).
4. Reference to 'eternal' or 'everlasting' life is made when conferring the gift of baptism, confirmation or ordination. The same terms also occur in the words of administration at the eucharist, in the pronouncement of absolution, and in the blessing of a bride and groom in marriage.
5. Cf. G. L. Prestige, *God in Patristic Thought* (SPCK, 1952) pp. 73–4; W. James, *The Varieties of Religious Experience* (1902; Fontana, 1963) p. 498; M. de Unamuno, *The Tragic Sense of Life* (1912; Fontana, 1967).
6. From the Nicene Creed.
7. R. Bultmann, 'New Testament and Mythology', in H. W. Bartsch, *Kerygma and Myth* (Harper, 1961) p. 39.
8. Ibid., p. 8.
9. Cited in W. Kaufmann, *The Faith of a Heretic* (Anchor, 1963) p. 95.

10. A. Flew and A. MacIntyre, *New Essays in Philosophical Theology* (SCM, 1963) p. 268.
11. W. Lippmann, *A Preface to Morals*, pp. 30–1, cited in Flew and MacIntyre, *New Essays*, p. 268.
12. H. A. Williams, *True Resurrection* (Mitchel Beazley, 1972) p. 4.
13. H. J. Richards, *Death and After* (Fount, 1980) p. 38.
14. N. Lash, *Theology on Dover Beach* (DLT, 1979) p. 165.
15. J. Moltmann, *The Crucified God* (SCM, 1973) p. 170. Note: Moltmann's position is notoriously obscure because of his exuberant but uncritical use of biblical imagery, which is combined with an insistence that the language of faith and hope is very different from the language of facts (cf. p. 173). One is therefore never sure about what he supposes to be the case, since one cannot ascertain which language he is speaking at the time. Consequently some suppose him to take a semi-fundamentalist position, while others believe there is a Godless void at the heart of his theology. Compare, for example, the discussion in John Hick, *Death and Eternal Life* (Collins, 1976) pp. 213–5, with the reviews by J. A. Baker and D. Cupitt in *Theology* for September 1978 and May 1980 respectively. See also S. Travis, *Christian Hope and the Future of Man* (Inter-Varsity Press, 1980) pp. 94–5.
16. E.g. Romans 8.10–11, cf. R. Bultmann, 'New Testament and Mythology' in Bartsch, *Kerygma and Myth*, pp. 38ff. and Richards, *Death and After*, pp. 30ff.
17. Romans 6.11; cf. also Colossians 2.12–30; 3.1ff.
18. Phillipians 3.10; 1.23; 1.21; 3.20.
19. 2 Corinthians 1.22; 5.5.
20. 1 Corinthians 15.36; 2 Corinthians 5.6; Phillipians 1.23.
21. 2 Timothy 2.16–18.
22. Williams, *True Resurrection*, pp. 34–48.
23. Ibid., pp. 42–4.
24. Bartsch, *Kerygma and Myth*, pp. 37–40.
25. J. Moltmann, *Theology of Hope* (SCM, 1967), p. 210.
26. Moltmann, *The Crucified God*, pp. 177–8; cf. in general pp. 166–178 and pp. 332–8 and see note 13 above.
27. Richards, *Death and After*, pp. 38–9.
28. Lash, *Theology on Dover Beach*, p. 78.
29. Matthew 28.6; Mark 16.6; Luke 24.3; John 20.7.
30. John 20.17; 20.27.
31. Luke 24.39, Acts 10.41; cf. Luke 24.43; John 21.13–5.
32. Luke 24.31; 24.36; John 20.19; 20.26.
33. Luke 24.16; John 21.4.
34. Matthew 28.17.
35. 1 Corinthians 15.50.
36. 1 Corinthians 6.13.
37. 1 Corinthians 15.14.
38. 1 Corinthians 15.36.
39. 1 Corinthians 15.42–4.
40. C. F. Evans, *Resurrection and the New Testament* (SCM, 1970) p. 64.
41. 1 Corinthians 15.8.
42. 1 Corinthians 15.44.
43. 1 Peter 3.18.

44. See notes 29 to 32 above and also Matthew 28.2; Luke 24.23; John 20.12.
45. Acts 1.3–4; Luke 24.49–53; Matthew 28.16; John 21.1.
46. Mary Magdalene only (John 20.1); Mary Magdalene and the other Mary (Matthew 28.1); Mary Magdalene, the other Mary and Salome (Mark 16.1); Mary Magdalene, the other Mary, Joanna and the other women (Luke 24.10).
47. Matthew 28.8; 'Mark' 16.10; Luke 24.24; John 20.4 (only John mentions the race to the tomb).
48. Mark 14.50; 15.40.
49. This conclusion would have to be modified if further scientific tests on the Turin Shroud were to support all the claims currently being made for it. If the shroud is definitively proven to be of first century provenance and if it came to be generally agreed that only the dematerialization of the body laid within it could account for the shroud's markings, this would indeed powerfully reinforce the empty tomb tradition. Mark's story of a deliberate silence on the part of the witnesses would then have to be revived to explain why Paul knew nothing of this tradition. But so far from supporting the resurrection hopes of Christians it would in fact undermine them by cutting the connection, which St Paul saw as very important, between what happened to Christ and what we may reasonably expect to happen to ourselves. On the other hand the prima facie evidence for the shroud's authenticity is impressive, so its vindication would not be an impossible outcome of the current research. cf. I. Wilson, *The Turin Shroud* (Penguin, 1978) pp. 1–94 and pp. 255–86 and Peter Jennings, *Face to Face with the Turin Shroud* (Mowbrays, 1978).
50. 1 Corinthians 15.3–4.
51. Acts 2.27; 13.35.
52. 2 Corinthians 5.3–4 I take the expression 'inner nature' from the RSV translation of 4.16. The Greek text literally means 'the inward of us'.
53. 1 Corinthians 15.51, Philippians 3.21; 2 Corinthians 5.1.
54. G. W. H. Lampe and D. M. MacKinnon, *The Resurrection* (Mowbrays, 1966) p. 45. Note: The concept of 'personality' was not available to Paul as it did not enter western thought till the 4th century. But like Lampe I believe it articulates Paul's thought well to describe resurrection in terms of personality being clothed with a new body.
55. 1 Corinthians 15.37–8.
56. C. F. Evans, *Resurrection and the New Testament*, pp. 11–40, P. Badham, *Christian Beliefs*, pp. 38–40.
57. G. R. Driver, *The Judaean Scrolls* (Blackwell, 1965) p. 75.
58. Mark 12.24–7.
59. *Doctrine in the Church of England* 1938 (SPCK, 1962), p. 209.
60. Cf. Badham, *Christian Beliefs*, chapter 5.
61. Ibid., chapters 4 and 5.
62. Justin, *Dialogue with Trypho*, chapter 5.
63. Jerome, *Letter 126*, para. 1.
64. D. Z. Phillips, *Death and Immortality* (Macmillan, 1970) p. 44.
65. Ibid., pp. 43–4.
66. Ibid., p. 55.
67. Ibid., p. 48.
68. N. Autton, *The Pastoral Care of the Dying* (SPCK, 1966).

69. J. Oldknow and A. D. Crakie, *The Priests' Book of Private Devotions* (1878). Revised by J. Stobart (Mowbrays, 1960).
70. Autton, *The Pastoral Care of the Dying*, pp. 98, 105.
71. Oldknow and Crakie, *Priests' Book*, pp. 488–91.
72. Oldknow and Crakie, *Priests' Book*, p. 492; Autton, *The Pastoral Care of the Dying*, p. 108.
73. Cf. *A Manual of Eastern Orthodox Prayers* (SPCK, 1962) pp. 26–7.
74. Lash, *Theology on Dover Beach*, p. 180.
75. E. Busch, *Karl Barth* (SCM, 1976), p. 488.
76. Tillich, *Systematic Theology*, vol. 3 (Nisbet, 1968) p. 437.
77. John 17.3.
78. Cf. Nelson's *Concordance*.
79. John 12.23–5.
80. 1 John 2.25.
81. Romans 6.23.
82. Romans 2.7; 2 Corinthians 4.17.
83. Matthew 19.16–29, Mark 10.17–30, Luke 10.25; 18.18–30.
84. 2 Timothy 2.10–11, Titus 3.7, Hebrews 9.15; 1 Peter 5.10; 2 Peter 1.11.
85. See notes 4 and 71 above.
86. Cf. Hick, *Death and Eternal Life*, p. 218.
87. Ibid., p. 218.
88. Ibid., p. 219.
89. N. Pittenger, *After Death, Life in God* (SCM, 1980) pp. 51, 64.
90. The 'Dies Irae' from the Requiem Mass. I have taken my translation both from the English version of the Roman Missal, and from the version given as Hymn no. 466 in Ancient and Modern Revised.
91. Pittenger, *After Death* p. 65.
92. In fact she wrote 'Tout comprendre rend très indulgent', but the translation I have given is the usual epitome of her thought. *The Oxford Dictionary of Quotations* gives the original form of Madame de Staël's remark.
93. D. Edwards, 'Where is heaven?' in R. S. Wright, *Asking them Questions* part II (OUP, 1972).
94. D. L. Edwards, *The Last Things Now* (SCM, 1969) p. 89; 2 Timothy 1.3–4.
95. M. de Unamuno, *The Tragic Sense of Life* (1912; Fontana, 1967) p. 154.
96. Edwards, *The Last Things Now*, p. 92.
97. From the *Good News Bible* (Fontana, 1976).
98. Cf. C. S. Peirce on 'Types and tokens', in *The Simplest Mathematics* in Collected Papers of C. S. Peirce, vol. IV (Belknap Press, 1960) p. 423, section 537.
99. Pittenger, *After Death*, p. 78.
100. K. Rahner, *Foundations of Christian Faith* (DLT, 1978) p. 444.
101. J. Macquarrie, *Christian Hope* (Mowbrays, 1978) p. 128, note 25.
102. N. Berdyaev, *The Destiny of Man* (Bles, 1955) p. 294.
103. Pittenger, *After Death* p. 64.
104. O. Cullmann has made a similar criticism of the concept of the immortality of the soul on the grounds that it is not compatible with the New Testament's position. The precise term athanasia (immortality) occurs twice: once in connection with man's destiny (1 Corinthians 15.53–4) and once referring to God alone (1 Timothy 6.16). However the concept of the immortality of the

soul is taken for granted by all the early Christian Fathers and was declared *de fide* for all Roman Catholics at the fifth Lateran Council. The Liturgical usages cited in this chapter show how deeply it has been incorporated into Christian tradition. cf. K. Stendahl, *Immortality and Resurrection* (Macmillan, 1965).

105. Pittenger, *After Death* p. 74; Nehemiah 13.31; Psalms 25.7; 112.6; Job 14.13.
106. 2 Peter 1.14; 1.11; 3.13.
107. Edwards, *The Last Things Now*, p. 91.
108. Revelation 21.4.

CHAPTER 3 : The Naturalistic Case for Extinction

1. I think that G. Santayana once wrote 'the fact of being born is a poor augury for immortality', but I have failed to track this down in his works.
2. In D. Hume, *On Religion*, ed. R. Wollheim (Fontana, 1963) pp. 267–8. This is a collection of extracts from Hume's writings.
3. Arnobius, *Against the Pagans* 2.7.
4. Oppenheimer, 'Life after Death' in *Theology*, (September 1979) p. 334.
5. Hick, *Death and Eternal Life* (Collins, 1976) p. 42.
6. A. S. Mason, *Health and Hormones* (Penguin, 1960) p. 48. V. H. Mottram, *The Physical Basis of Personality* (Penguin, 1944) p. 74.
7. Mottram, *The Physical Basis of Personality*, p. 78. The blood stream will never actually go short of calcium because of lack of intake, for the parathyroids will, if working normally always make up deficiencies by drawing on the bones even at the expense of so weakening the bones that they snap. Consequently lack of calcium in the blood is due to failure of the parathyroids to function correctly. Cf. Mason, *Health and Hormones*, pp. 86–96.
8. Mottram, *The Physical Basis of Personality* p. 86.
9. Mottram, *The Physical Basis of Personality*, pp. 95–96. Readers' Digest, *Family Health Guide* (Readers' Digest, 1972) p. 94.
10. In his Editorial Foreword to Mason, *Health and Hormones* p. 7.
11. Mottram, *The Physical Basis of Personality*, p. 71.
12. Cf. P. Badham, *Christian Beliefs about Life after Death* (Macmillan, 1976) chapter 7.
13. The *Lancet*, 26 January 1980, Vol. 1, p. 167.
14. J. N. D. Anderson, *Issues of Life and Death* (Hodder, 1976) p. 66.
15. R. F. R. Gardner, *Abortion, the Personal Dilemma* (Paternoster, 1972) p. 124.
16. Gardner, *Abortion*, p. 123; A Smith, *The Body* (Penguin, 1978) p. 243.
17. Smith, *The Body*, p. 168.
18. *Abortion, an Ethical Discussion* (Church Information Office, 1965) p. 35, note 1.
19. S. Rose, *The Conscious Brain* (Penguin, 1976).
20. R. S. Lee, *Your Growing Child and Religion* (Penguin, 1965) pp. 28–9.
21. Rose, *The Conscious Brain*, pp. 202, 194.
22. Smith, *The Body*, p. 342.
23. C. Blakemore, *Mechanics of the mind* (CUP, 1977) p. 141 for Japan; Smith, *The Body*, p. 349 for British Law. Cf. R. Goldman, *Readiness for Religion* (RKP, 1964).
24. Smith, *The Body*, p. 332. According to Smith the births of 315,456 babies were

registered in London between the years 1730 and 1749. Of this number 74.5 per cent died before the age of five. Only by the end of the eighteenth century did more survive than die during the first five years. J. Morley in *Death, Heaven and the Victorians* shows that in Manchester, mortality before the age of five was still running at 57 per cent of working class children in 1840.

25. Hick, *Death and Eternal Life*, p. 153.
26. S. George, *How the Other Half Dies* (Penguin, 1977) p. 31.
27. C. Sagan, *The Dragons of Eden: speculations on the evolution of human intelligence* (Hodder, 1978) p. 98.
28. C. Blakemore, *Mechanics of the mind*, pp. 178–81; Rose, *The Conscious Brain*, p. 319–20; I. Ramsey, *Biology and Personality* (Blackwell, 1965) pp. 139–49; M. Williams, *Brain Damage and the Mind* (Penguin, 1970); K. R. Popper and J. C. Eccles, *The Self and its Brain* (Springer International, 1977) pp. 296, 483.
29. M. A. Simpson, *The Facts of Death* (Prentice Hall, 1979) p. 46.
30. Penguin, 1972.
31. Augustine, *City of God*, Bk. 22, chapters 14 and 15.
32. Hume, *On Religion*, p. 269.
33. A Farrer, *Love Almighty and Ills Unlimited* (Fontana, 1966) p. 190.
34. J. Glover, *Causing Death and Saving Lives* (Penguin, 1977) p. 126.
35. I. Asimov, *Guide to Science vol. 2* (Penguin, 1972) p. 349.
36. R. Leakey, *Origins* (Macdonald and Jane's, 1977) p. 88.
37. Leakey, *Origins*, chapter 5.
38. Sagan, *The Dragons of Eden*, pp. 88–91; Leakey, *Origins*, pp. 86, 90, 110, 112, 205.
39. Sagan, *The Dragons of Eden*, p. 88; Leakey, *Origins*, chapter 5.
40. Leakey, *Origins*, p. 52.
41. Hume, *On Religion*, p. 264.
42. Cited in M. Midgley, *Beast and Man* (Methuen, 1979) p. 211, from Descartes 'Discourse 5', cf. (in another translation) R. Descartes, *Discourse on Method and other writings* (Penguin, 1968) p. 75.
43. J. Huxley, *The Uniqueness of Man* (Chatto and Windus, 1941) p. 16.
44. T. Dobzhansky, 'Chance and Creativity in Evolution', in F. J. Ayala and T. Dobzhansky (eds), *Studies in the Philosophy of Biology* (University of California, 1974) p. 334.
45. Ibid., p. 333.
46. E.g. G. G. Simpson, J. Bronowski, S. L. Washburn *et al.* cited in E. Linden, *Apes, Men and Language* (Penguin, 1974) p. 50.
47. Cf. Linden, *Apes, Men and Language*, pp. 224–31.
48. W. H. Thorpe, 'Reductionism in Biology', in Ayala and Dobzhansky *Studies in the Philosophy of Biology*, p. 129.
49. Linden, *Apes, Men and Language*, pp. 105–13.
50. Midgley, *Beast and Man*, p. 227.
51. Midgley, *Beast and Man*, p. 351, cf. Popper and Eccles, *The Self and its Brain*, p. 445.
52. R. M. Lockley, *Whales, dolphins and porpoises* (David and Charles, 1979) pp. 48–51. Asimov, *Guide to Science*, p. 379; Midgley, *Beast and Man*, p. 229. Note: Sir John Eccles argues that when dolphins' brains are studied anatomically it seems that a good deal of their cerebral hemispheres are used in auditory localization, so we cannot really know yet how to interpret the fact that they

have such large brains (Popper and Eccles, *The Self and its Brain*, p. 445). In terms of brain to body weight the dolphin is man's only rival among animals of any significant size.

CHAPTER 4 :   The Attenuation of Doctrinal Support for Belief in a Future Life

1. N. Lash, *Theology on Dover Beach* (DLT, 1979) pp. vi, and 181–2.
2. Genesis 1 and 2 passim. Cf. especially 1.17. I cite the *Good News Bible* translation. G. Von Rad points out that the word translated 'lights' is simply the ordinary word for a household lamp (Genesis, SCM 1963, p. 53). Incorporating this into the NEB translation we would then read 'God put these lamps in the vault of heaven to give light on earth'. This description of the stars really does bring out the geocentric, man-orientated vision of the author of Genesis!
3. For a fuller description see A. D. White, *A history of the warfare of science with theology* (1894; Arco, 1955) p. 118.
4. Cited by Sir Bernard Lovell in his article 'Creation' in *Theology*, vol. LXXXIII, no. 695 (September 1980) p. 360.
5. Cited by Pope John-Paul II in his *Sign of Contradiction* (Hodder, 1979) p. 19.
6. Cf. for example the Prayer of Thanksgiving in Series II of the C of E or the Collect for Trinity 23 in Series III. See also The Great Thanksgiving, and the Collects for Christmas 1 and Septuagesima in the modern Eucharist of the Church in Wales first published in September 1980. For Catechisms: see R. Lawler, D. W. Wuerl and T. C. Lawler, *The Teaching of Christ* (Veritas, 1976) chapters 3 and 4 for a very strongly commended Catholic Catechism; and see W. G. Wilson, *The Faith of an Anglican* (Fount, 1980) pp. 35ff. for an equally highly commended Anglican one. That this perspective is also shared by the Free Churches: see the agreed document produced by all the denominations involved in the Nationwide Initiative on Evangelism printed in *The Times* (28 July 1980).
7. Cf. the Anglican rites cited in note 6 above.
8. The most famous presentation of this is St. Anselm's profoundly influential work, *Why God became Man (Cur Deus Homo)*.
9. E. L. Mascall, *The Importance of Being Human* (OUP, 1959) p. 22.
10. *Sign of Contradiction*, p. 102.
11. Numerous references may be found in V. Lossky, *The Mystical Theology of the Eastern Church* (James Clarke, 1957) chapter 7.
12. Cf. Athanasius, *Orations* 1.39, *On the Incarnation*, chapter 54 and references as in note 11 above.
13. Lossky, *The Mystical Theology*, p. 153.
14. J. S. Bezzant, 'Intellectual Objections', in A. R. Vidler, *Objections to Christian Belief* (Constable, 1963) p. 84.
15. Sir Bernard Lovell, 'Creation', p. 362.
16. R. Jastrow, *Until the Sun Dies* (Fontana, 1977) p. 18.
17. BBC2 Monday 15 September 1980; cf. *Radio Times* (13–19 September 1980).
18. Cf. Vatican II, *Pastoral Constitution on the Church in the Modern World*, chapter 3, 'Man's activity in the Universe', para. 39. A. Flannery, *Vatican Council II* (Dominion, 1977) p. 938, and *The Teaching of Christ* (see ref. 6 above) pp. 68–9.

Although this appears explicitly in the context of an exposition of Genesis 1, I cite it because the authors describe this passage as teaching 'essential truths about humanity'.

19. For discussion of how many planets might contain intelligent life see R. Puccetti, *Persons* (Macmillan, 1968) chapters 3 and 4 and I. Asimov, *Extraterrestrial Civilisations* (Robson Books, 1980).
20. Lovell estimates 10,000 million, Jastrow doubles it.
21. C. Sagan, *The Dragons of Eden: speculations on the evolution of human intelligence* (Hodder, 1978) pp. 14–6.
22. John-Paul II, *Redemptor Hominis* (CTS, 1979) p. 3.
23. D. Cupitt, *The Debate about Christ* (SCM, 1979) p. 37.
24. Mascall, *The Importance of Being Human*, p. 14.
25. Jastrow, *Until the Sun Dies*, p. 15.
26. Lovell, 'Creation', pp. 363–4.
27. E.g. S. Weinberg, *The First Three Minutes* (Deutsch, 1977) p. 155. P. Davies, *The Runaway Universe* (Dent, 1978) p. 31. For a judicious theological survey see A. R. Peacocke, *Creation and the World of Science* (CUP, 1979).
28. For a modern philosophical defence of the probable existence of a divine creator see R. Swinburne, *The Existence of God* (Clarendon, 1979).
29. *A Hundred Hymns for Today* (W. Clowes, 1969) no. 21. See also no. 3, 'All my hope on God is founded', verse 3, and hymn 666 in *Songs of Praise* (OUP, 1949), 'There's a wideness in God's mercy', verse 3.
30. Puccetti, *Persons*, p. 65. See also note 19 above.
31. E. L. Mascall, *Christian Theology and Natural Science* (Longmans, Green, 1956) p. 43.
32. See note 9 above.
33. It ought to be noted that this reinterpretation of the fall is profoundly unfair to animals. For real evil we should observe the behaviour of our own species. Cf. Mary Midgley, *Beast and Man* (Methuen, 1980) for illustration of this.
34. Colossians 1.19; 2.9.
35. Cf. The Prayer Book Collect for Advent 1. 'Thy Son Jesus Christ came to visit us'.
36. Mascall shows that it is logically possible to reconcile the classical formularies of Christology with multiple simultaneous incarnations in many worlds. But it would be very hard to see how this reconciliation of the technical formulas could be expressed in the normal vocabulary of Christian teaching. Cf. *Christian Theology and Natural Science*, p. 41.
37. C. Longley, 'Christianity retreating in spite of education in schools', *The Times*, (25 September 1978).
38. This view was championed by Benjamin Jowett in his *Commentaries on the Epistles of St. Paul* of 1855. One point in its favour is that no fully developed theory of the atonement was put forward before St. Anselm in the 11th century, and the theory of penal substitution is not clearly found before the 16th century reformers. But there is considerable debate about this issue in contemporary New Testament scholarship. M. Hengel seeks to oppose the increasing strength of this view in his latest book, *The Atonement* (SCM, 1981).
39. Cf. J. Hick, *The Myth of God Incarnate* (SCM, 1977) p. 171; J. A. Baker, *The Foolishness of God* (DLT, 1970) pp. 143ff.

40. F. D. E. Schleiermacher, *The Christian Faith* (T. and T. Clark, 1960) pp. 391–402.
41. Cf. D. Cupitt, *Crisis of Moral Authority* (Lutterworth, 1972) chapter 1.
42. Cf. The Collect for the Second Sunday after Christmas or in Series III the Third Collect for Christmas Day.
43. This description is collated from Matthew chapter 25, verses 32, 34 and 46 and Revelation 20.10 and 21.8.
44. D. Hume, 'On the Immortality of the Soul' 1777, reprinted in D. Hume, *On Religion* (Fontana, 1963) p. 266.
45. H. B. Wilson, 'The National Church', in B. Jowett, *Essays and Reviews* (Oxford, 1860) pp. 205–6.
46. R. S. Peters, *Ethics and Education* (Unwin, 1966) p. 272.
47. Ibid., p. 273.
48. U. Bronfenbrenner, *Two Worlds of Childhood* (Allen and Unwin, 1970) pp. 10ff.
49. J. Hick, *Death and Eternal Life* (Collins, 1976) p. 202.
50. Unless of course purgatory be taken to *replace* hell. But in the traditional schema purgatory is for those destined for heaven, it is not seen as an escape route from hell but only as a probation for heaven.
51. Hume, *On Religion*, p. 266.
52. F. W. Newman, *Life after Death?* (1886) p. 34, cited in G. Rowell, *Hell and the Victorians* (Clarendon, 1974) p. 59.
53. Hick, *The Myth of God Incarnate*, p. 203.
54. Ibid., pp. 205–7, cf. pp. 442–6.
55. Tertullian, *De Spectaculis* chapter 30, cited in W. R. Alger, *The Destiny of the Soul* 1860 (Greenwood Press, 1968) p. 513.
56. P. Lombard, *Sentences* 4/50/7, cited in P. Dearmer, *The Legend of Hell* (Cassell, 1929) p. 34.
57. F. L. Cross, *Oxford Dictionary of the Christian Church* (OUP, 1963) pp. 1054–5.
58. St. Thomas Aquinas, *Summa Theologiae*, Pt. III, Supp. 94, art 1, cited in A. Flew, *God and Philosophy* (Hutchinson, 1966) p. 57 and Dearmer, *The Legend of Hell*, p. 35.
59. Dearmer, *The Legend of Hell*, p. 35.
60. Ibid., p. 25.
61. Cf. Alger, *The Destiny of the Soul*, Pt. 5, chapter 4; Dearmer, *The Legend of Hell*, chapter 1; G. Rowell, *Hell and the Victorians*, chapter 2; F. W. Farrar, *Eternal Hope* (1878; Macmillan, 1912) chapter 3; J. Pohle and A. Preuss, *Eschatology* 1917 (Greenwood Press, 1971) chapter 4. Note: This differs from the other books because its authors still believe in the doctrine, and suppose that the picture they give of the pains of hell corresponds to reality. This book also has (or had) considerable standing in the R. C. Church as a presentation of official Catholic teaching.
62. W. E. H. Lecky, *History of the Rise and Influence of the Spirit of Rationalism in Europe*, vol. I, pp. 329, 327; vol. II, p. 36, cited in Dearmer, *The Legend of Hell*, p. 67.
63. Alger, *The Destiny of the Soul*, p. 515.
64. Dearmer, *The Legend of Hell*, pp. 39–40, 68–9; Alger, *The Destiny of the Soul*, pp. 512–5.
65. B. Russell, *Why I am not a Christian* (1957; Unwin, 1975) p. 24.
66. D. Cupitt, *Crisis of Moral Authority* (Lutterworth, 1972) p. 77.
67. Dearmer, *The Legend of Hell*, pp. 71–2.

68. I. Bradley, *The Call to Seriousness* (Cape, 1976) p. 188.
69. J. A. Motyer, *After Death* (Hodder, 1965) p. 27.
70. Ibid., p. 40.
71. Ibid., p. 38.
72. Ibid., pp. 36, 46, 47.
73. Ibid., p. 35.
74. Ibid., p. 38. Incidentally this is a quotation from Isaiah 55.8 and the prophet continues, 'for my ways are *higher* than your ways, and my thoughts than your thoughts'.
75. From J. S. Mill, *Three Essays*, London 1874 cited in Dearmer, *The Legend of Hell*, p. 114. A variant of this from Mill's 1865 *Examination of Sir William Hamilton's Philosophy*, p. 103, is more commonly quoted: 'I will call no being good, who is not what I mean when I apply that epithet to my fellow creatures'. cf. Rowell, *Hell and the Victorians*, p. 3.
76. In practice he will probably not be willing since persons with a 'high' doctrine of revelation frequently suppose God to have 'revealed' truths which human reason finds incompatible. But the law of the excluded middle does not cease to apply because we choose to ignore it. The claim that both p and not-p are equally true remains meaningless even if we take p to be the divinely revealed truth that God is love.
77. Cf. Hick, *The Myth of God Incarnate*, chapter 13.
78. Matthew 25.31–46; Luke 16.19–31.
79. G. Bornkamm, *Jesus of Nazareth* (Hodder, 1960) p. 128; C. H. Dodd, *The Founder of Christianity* (Collins, 1971) chapter 4.
80. Vidler, *Objections to Christian Belief*, p. 84; cf. note 14.
81. Pope John-Paul II, *Sign of Contradiction* (Hodder, 1979) p. 180. It should be stressed that this is a very tentative paragraph, and it is possible that on the next page his discussion could be interpreted as going back on this position, but since he insists that 'God *will* be all in all' it is very hard to be sure, especially as a papal letter defending Hell was issued in July 1979.
82. Cf. the examples given of earlier total confidence in J. Hick, 'Towards a Theology of Death' in his *God and the Universe of Faiths* (Macmillan, 1973).
83. M. Hammerton and A. C. Downing, 'Fringe beliefs among undergraduates' in *Theology*, vol. LXXXII, no 690 (November 1979) pp. 433–6.
84. Thus the question of hell dominated all 19th century discussions of the future life. Cf. the works by Alger and Farrar whereas modern twentieth century discussions such as those of Hick or my own earlier work only refer to hell in passing.
85. W. James, *The Varieties of Religious Experience* (1902; Fontana, 1963) p. 498.
86. M. Unamuno, *The Tragic Sense of Life* (1912; Fontana, 1967).

CHAPTER 5: The Evidence from near-Death Experiences

1. R. A. Moody, *Life after Life* (1975; Bantam Books, 1977); J. C. Hampe, *To Die is Gain* (1975; DLT, 1979).
2. M. A. Simpson, *The Facts of Death* (Prentice Hall, 1979) p. 32.
3. On the cover of Moody's book. Note that Dr Moody explicitly denies that he is

'trying to construct a proof of survival of bodily death' (p. 182), even though he regards the data as 'highly significant' for such a belief.

4. In her foreword to Moody's book.
5. P. Kurtz, 'Is there life after death?', a paper submitted to the Eighth International Conference on the Unity of the Sciences, Los Angeles November 1979.
6. Hampe, *To Die is Gain*, pp. 47 and 50. Rosalind Heywood, 'Attitudes to Death in the light of dreams and other "out-of-the-body" experience', in A. Toynbee, *Man's Concern with Death* (Hodder, 1968) p. 196.
7. Sir Cyril Burt, *Psychology and Psychical Research* (Society for Psychical Research, 1968) pp. 79–80.
8. Ibid.
9. R. G. Druss and D. S. Kornfield, 'The survivors of cardiac arrest', in the *Journal of the American Medical Association*, vol. 201 (31 July 1967) pp. 295 and 293.
10. E. Garth Moore, *Believe it or not* (Mowbrays, 1977) p. 57.
11. Druss and Kornfield, '*The survivors of cardiac arrest*', p. 293; B. M. Dlin, A. Stern and S. J. Poliakoff, 'Survivors of cardiac arrest', *Journal of Psychosomatics*, vol. 15, (1974) pp. 63–4.
12. Reported in the *Observer*, (8 April 1979).
13. Cited in M. Ebon, *The Evidence for Life after Death* (Signet, 1977) p. 44.
14. Hampe, *To Die is Gain*, chapter 3.
15. R. A. Moody, *Reflections on Life after Life* (Corgi, 1978)p. 110.
16. Cited in R. Crookall, *What Happens when you Die* (Colin Smythe, 1978) pp. 18–19.
17. C. D. Broad, *Lectures on Psychical Research* (RKP, 1962) p. 169ff.; R. A. Moody, *Reflections*, p. 110; Geddes cited in Toynbee, *Man's Concern with Death*, p. 196 and in G. N. M. Tyrrell, *The Personality of Man*, (Penguin, 1948) pp. 198–9; Hampe, *To Die is Gain*, p. 47. See also C. J. Ducasse, *The Belief in a Life after Death* (Charles Thomas, 1961) p. 162; R. Johnson, *The Imprisoned Splendour* (Hodder, 1969) p. 223; C. Fiore and A. Landsburg, *Death Encounters* (Bantam, 1979) p. 33.
18. As note 17, especially Broad, Moody, Hampe, Ducasse and Fiore; also Burt, *Psychology*, p. 81 and Garth Moore, *Believe it or Not*, p. 57.
19. Burt, *Psychology*, p. 79.
20. *Parapsychology Review*, vol. 9, no. 2, (March–April 1978) p. 17. Persons willing to share information about claimed near-death experiences should write to Dr Ian Stevenson, Box 152, Medical Center, University of Virginia, Charlottesville, Virginia 22901, USA.
21. W. G. Roll, 'A new look at the survival problem', in J. Beloff, *New Directions in Parapsychology* (Elek, 1974) pp. 150–1.
22. Cf. Beloff, *New Directions in Parapsychology*, p. 150 for Roll's explanation of this. 'It is seldom, however, that people can induce out of the body experiences on demand'.
23. C. Tart, 'Out-of-the-body experiences' in E. D. Mitchell, *Psychic Exploration* (Putnam, 1974) p. 361.
24. K. Osis, 'New ASPR research of out-of-the-body experiences', *Newsletter of American Society for Psychical Research*, no. 14, (Summer 1972). Cited in A. Spraggett, *The Case for Immortality* (Signet, 1974) p. 82.

25. K. Osis and J. L. Mitchell, 'Physiological correlates of reported out-of-the-body experiences', in the *SPR Journal*, vol. 49, no 772, (June 1977) p. 525.
26. C. Tart in *ASPR Journal*, (January 1968) cited in Spraggett, *The Case for Immortality*, p. 81.
27. C. Tart in Osis and Mitchell, 'physiological correlates', p. 354.
28. Susan Blackmore, *Parapsychology and out-of-the-body experiences* (Transpersonal Books, 1978) p. 16.
29. Ibid., p. 18.
30. Ibid., pp. 19–20.
31. Ibid., p. 19.
32. Osis and Mitchell, 'Physiological correlates', p. 526.
33. Moody, *Life after Death*, p. 96.
34. E. Kubler Ross, 'Death does not exist', *Coevolution Quarterly*, (Summer 1977) p. 103.
35. Cited in Fiore and landsburg, *Death Encounters*, p. 15.
36. The *Observer* (8 April 1979).
37. Cf. R. Swinburne, *The Existence of God* (Clarendon, 1979) chapter 13 for an interesting development of this argument.
38. G. Kliman, 'The child faces his own death', in A. H. Kutscher, *Death and Bereavement* (Charles C. Thomas, 1974) p. 21.
39. Kubler Ross, 'Death does not exist', p. 104.
40. I owe this argument to my colleague, Professor C. J. Lofmark.
41. Kubler Ross, 'Death does not exist', p. 104. We might also ask whether it is conceivable that in twelve years of life a child would never have learnt that its parents had previously had another child who had died.
42. Dr Thomas Smith, 'Called back from the dead', in *Pulse*, (19 July 1980).
43. Sir William Barrett, *Death-bed Visions* (Methuen, 1926) p. 1.
44. Kubler Ross, 'Death does not exist', p. 104; Spraggett, *The Case for Immortality*, p. 95.
45. J. F. McHarg reviewing *At the Hour of Death* in the *Journal of the Society for Psychical Research*, vol. 49, no 777, pp. 885–7.
46. Moody, *Life after Life*, p. 157.
47. Cf. S. Grof and J. Halifax, *The Human Encounter with death* (Condor, 1977) p. 142.
48. Title of article in *Psychiatry*, vol. 39, 1976; cf. Ebon, *The Evidence for Life After Death*, p. 34.
49. R. Noyes, 'The Experience of Dying', *Psychiatry*, vol. 35, (May 1972) p. 178.
50. Ibid., pp. 179–180.
51. M. A. Simpson, *The Facts of Death*, pp. 33–5.
52. K. Osis and E. Haraldsson, *At the Hour of Death* (Avon, 1977) chapter 3.
53. K. Osis, *Deathbed Observations of Physicians and Nurses* (Parapsychology Foundation, 1961) pp. 84–5.
54. Osis and Haraldsson, *At the Hour of Death*, p. 84.
55. Ibid., p. 78.
56. Ibid., p. 88.
57. Ibid., p. 91.
58. Osis, *Deathbed observations*, pp. 84–5; Osis and Haraldsson, *At the Hour of Death*, pp. 84–8.
59. Fiore and Landsburg, *Death Encounters*, p. 13.

60. Most of these data in the *Lancet* actually come from R. G. Druss and D. S. Kornfield (cf. note 9 above). Their article is based on ten male survivors of cardiac arrest so 80 per cent actually means eight of the ten! The 'I am dead syndrome' is reported in an article by B. M. Dlin and others (cf. note 11 above).

61. M. Rawlings, *Beyond Death's Door* (Sheldon, 1978) p. 21; cf. also pp. 64–6.

62. Hampe, *To Die is Gain*, p. 51.

63. Simpson, *The Facts of Death*, pp. 32–5.

64. D. Shiels, 'A cross-cultural study of beliefs in out-of-the-body experiences', *Journal of the Society for Psychical Research*, vol. 49, no 775, (March 1978) p. 697.

65. Ibid., p. 699.

66. BBC Radio 3 discussion on *Life after Life*, 20 June 1980.

67. Moody, *Reflections*, pp. 66–8.

68. Bede, *A History of the English Church and People* 731 A.D. (Penguin, 1962) Bk 5, chapter 12, pp. 284–9; see also pp. 289–293.

69. Osis and Haraldsson, Grof and Halifax, and Moody all obtain her support in this way.

70. W. Kaufmann, 'On death and lying', in *Existentialism, Religion and Death* (New American Library, 1976) p. 220.

71. Kubler Ross, 'Death does not exist', p. 107.

72. G. N. M. Tyrrell, *Apparitions* (Duckworth, 1953) p. 54.

73. Cited as preface to R. Crookall, *What Happens when you Die*.

74. C. S. King, *Psychic and Religious Phenomena* (Greenwood Press, 1978).

75. Moody, *Observer*, (8 April 1979); Kubler Ross, private letter dated 30 June 1978.

CHAPTER 6: The Evidence from Psychical Research

1. C. D. Broad, *Religion, Philosophy and Psychical Research* (RKP, 1953) p. 1.

2. C. D. Broad, *Lectures on Psychical Research* (RKP, 1962) pp. 3–4.

3. Cf. P. Badham, *Christian Beliefs about Life after Death* (Macmillan, 1976) pp. 113–24.

4. C. E. M. Hansel, *ESP a scientific evaluation* (Macgibbon and Kee, 1966) pp. 114–6, 234–5; cf. Badham, *Christian Beliefs*, p. 115.

5. Cited in E. D. Mitchell, *Psychic Exploration* (Putnam, 1974) p. 47.

6. J. G. Pratt, 'In search of the consistent scorer', in J. Beloff, *New Directions in Parapsychology* (Elek, 1974) chapter 5.

7. C. Honorton and S. Krippner, 'Hypnosis and ESP performance' in R. A. White, *Surveys in Parapsychology* (Scarecrow Press, 1976) p. 255. (Note Hansel, p. 173, for early criticism of Stepanek and compare with p. 257 of Honorton and Krippner and with Beloff's introduction to Pratt, 'In search of the consistent scorer').

8. Badham, *Christian Beliefs*, p. 116; cf. L. L. Vasiliev, *Experiments in mental suggestion* (Galley Hull Press, 1963).

9. Badham, *Christian Beliefs*, pp. 114–15.

10. M. Welman in introduction to E. D. Mitchell, *Psychic Exploration* (Putnam's, 1974) p. 47.

11. K. Campbell, *Body and Mind* (Macmillan, 1970) p. 91.

12. For discussion of this point, cf. H. D. Lewis, *Persons and Life after Death* (Macmillan, 1978).
13. There are difficulties with this position. Identical twins appear to have the strongest sense of telepathic rapport which suggests that a material basis for telepathy might yet be found. And alleged evidence for telepathic rapport between man and animals (e. g. horses, dogs and dolphins) reminds us of the problem that even on a dualist account of mentality, it is hard to draw an absolute line between man and other animals. For evidence of animal ESP see J. Randall, 'Biological Aspects of Psi', in J. Beloff, *New Directions in Parapsychology*, and in G. N. M. Tyrrell, *Apparitions* (Duckworth, 1953) pp. 76–7.
14. R. H. Thouless, 'Theories about survival', *Journal of the Society for Psychical Research*, vol. 50, no. 779, (March 1979) p. 2.
15. K. Osis and E. Haraldsson, *At the Hour of Death* (Avon, 1977) pp. 13–14.
16. W. D. Rees, 'The Hallucinations of Widowhood', BMJ, 4, (1971) pp. 37–41.
17. Osis and Haraldsson, *At the Hour of Death*, pp. 13–14.
18. G. N. M. Tyrrell, *Apparitions*, p. 19.
19. Ibid., p. 21.
20. F. W. H. Myers, *Human Personality* (Longmans, Green, 1909) p. 227.
21. Augustine's story may be read in Michael Perry, *The Resurrection of Man* (Mowbrays, 1975) pp. 21–2.
22. For a full account of this case see, C. D. Broad, *Lectures on Psychical Research*, pp. 137–9.
23. C. E. M. Hansel, *ESP: a scientific evaluation*, pp. 228–9.
24. Cf. M. Perry, *The Resurrection of Man*, pp. 28–9.
25. R. Heywood, 'Death and Psychical Research', in A. Toynbee, *Man's concern with death* (Hodder, 1968) p. 233.
26. This description of the cross-correspondences owes much to R. Heywood, *The Sixth Sense* (Chatto and Windus, 1959) chapters 8 and 9.
27. G. N. M. Tyrrell, *The Personality of Man* (Penguin, 1948) pp. 145–6.
28. Mrs Fleming is known in the earlier literature as Mrs Holland, a pseudonym which she used because her relatives did not approve of her involvement with this research.
29. Cf. Tyrrell, *The Personality of Man*, p. 146.
30. Heywood. *The Sixth Sense*, p. 73.
31. W. H. Salter, *Zoar: The Evidence of Psychical Research Concerning Survival* (Sidgwick and Jackson, 1961), p. 207.
32. Cited in F. H. Saltmarsh, *The Evidence of Personal Survival from Cross-correspondences* (Bell, 1938) p. 141.
33. G. Murphy, *The Challenge of Psychical Research* (Harpers, 1961) p. 271.
34. Ibid., p. 273.

CHAPTER 7:   Claimed Memories of Former Lives

1. Cf. J. Iverson, *More Lives than One?* (Pan, 1977) p. 24.
2. I. Stevenson, *Cases of Reincarnation Type*, vol. 1 *Ten Cases in India* (Univ. Press of Virginia, 1975) p. 1.
3. Dr. John Beloff, for example, describes Stevenson as 'unquestionably one of the

most intellectually distinguished persons at present working in the field of parapsychology. He is a person of unimpeachable integrity and judgement'. JSPR (1967) p. 89.

4. I. Stevenson, *Twenty Cases Suggestive of Reincarnation* (ASPR 1966) pp. 20–33.

5. Ibid., pp. 23–30.

6. Ibid., p. 320.

7. Ibid., p. 119.

8. Ibid., p. 64.

9. Ibid., pp. 257, 271.

10. Ibid., p. 290.

11. Ibid., pp. 257, 271.

12. Ibid., pp. 273–4.

13. Ibid., p. 5.

14. Ibid., p. 324.

15. Stevenson, *Cases of Reincarnation Type*, p. 143.

16. Cf. the case of Jagdish Chandra, ibid., pp. 172–5.

17. Stevenson, *Twenty cases*, pp. 49 and viii.

18. It is not uncommon to find champions of reincarnation attributing falsely such beliefs to various of the early Christian Fathers, and even to philosophers like Hume and Kant. cf. discussion of this point in J. Hick, *Death and Eternal Life* (Collins, 1976) pp. 392 ff., notes 2 and 16 where Hick criticises Weatherhead. Note also the quotations from Hume and Kant cited by C. J. Ducasse, *The Belief in Life After Death* (Springfield, 1961) p. 216.
A comparison with the original contexts shows the extent to which these quotations are misrepresentations of their authors' overall positions.

19. The pseudonym of Virginia Burns Tighe.

20. J. Iverson, *More Lives than One?*

21. Ibid.

22. Cf. ibid., pp. 24, 119; also Arthur Guirdham, *The Cathars and Reincarnation* (Neville Spearman, 1970) p. 89.

23. Cf. Iverson, *More Lives than One?* pp. 43–6, 83.

24. I. Stevenson, *The Evidence for Survival from claimed Memories of Former Incarnations* (ASPR reprint, 1961) p. 40.

25. For example, at least two of Mrs Evans other 'personnae' gave faulty information. Thus 'Alison' seemed not to know that her master, Jacques Coeur, was married. (Iverson, *More Lives than One?*, pp. 68, 62 ff.) 'Livonia' made reference to Roman ladies riding on horseback rather than in carriages. (Iverson, p. 58.) Again, Guirdham's subject reported being the mistress of a Cathar 'priest'. This seems intrinsically incredible, partly because Cathars rejected a set-apart priesthood, and also because their 'parfaits' were those who had succeeded in 'perfecting detachment from' the temptations of the flesh. Moreover they risked – and usually suffered – the unspeakable tortures of the inquisition in loyalty to their beliefs and ascetic practices. Why anyone should *pretend* to be a Cathar parfait at such an appalling risk beggars the imagination! (cf. Guirdham, *The Cathars and Reincarnation*, p. 92.)

26. Cf. Iverson, *More Lives than One?*, p. 47.

27. Ibid., p. 141.

28. Ibid., p. 142; cf. A. Spraggett, *The Case for Immortality* (Signet, 1975) p. 140.

29. I do not count 'Livonia's' references to York as 'Eboracum' and to Bath as

'Aqua Sulis' as the ability to speak Latin. This is just the sort of minimal linguistic data which English language histories or novels might supply.

30. This is to be contrasted with recitative xenoglossy where the subject is able to reproduce only a limited number of phrases in the foreign language and cannot converse in it.
31. Stevenson, *The Evidence for Survival*, p. 42.
32. Cf. section on Stevenson in J. Head and S. L. Cranston, (compilers and editors), *Reincarnation: the Phoenix Fire Mystery* (Julian Press, 1966) pp. 437–9.
33. L. Weatherhead, *The Christian Agnostic* (Hodder and Stoughton, 1967) pp. 248–9.
34. Iverson, *More Lives than One?*, p. 138.
35. Cf. Head and Cranston, *Reincarnation*, pp. 398–401; Christine Hartley, *A Case for Reincarnation* (Robert Hale, 1972) pp. 133 ff.
36. Guirdham, *The Cathars and Reincarnation*, p. 48.
37. Ibid., pp. 46, 135.
38. Ibid., p. 47.
39. E. S. Zolick, 'An Experimental Investigation of the Psychodynamic Implications of the Hypnotic 'Previous Existence' Fantasy', *J. Clin. Psychol.*, *14*, (1958) pp. 179–183.
40. Iverson, *More Lives than One?*, pp. 45–6; A. Guirdham, p. 92.
41. Cf. Iverson, *More Lives than One?*, p. 59.
42. Zolick, '*An Experimental Investigation*', p. 179.
43. Cf. Stevenson, *The Evidence for Survival*, p. 25, in which he cites Rosen's case of a young man who had unconsciously retained a few phrases of Oscan from a book which happened to be open on his table in a library.
44. Stevenson also contrasts in some detail various cryptomnesia cases with subjects claiming verifiably correct spontaneous waking memories. cf. Stevenson, *Twenty cases*, pp. 293–304.
45. Cf. Stevenson, *The Evidence for Survival*, pp. 28 ff.; and Stevenson, *Twenty cases*, pp. 305 ff.
46. Stevenson, *Twenty cases*, pp. 339–40.
47. Ibid., p. 340.
48. Stevenson, *The Evidence for Survival*, p. 43.

CHAPTER 8:   Immortality or Extinction?

1. G. Murphy, *The Challenge of Psychical Research* (Harper, 1961) p. 271.
2. C. D. Broad, *Lectures on Psychical Research* (RKP, 1962) p. 14.
3. Cited in R. Heywood, 'Notes on Changing Mental Climates', in J. R. Smythies, *Science and ESP* (RKP, 1967) p. 48.
4. Cited in J. Head and S. L. Cranston, *Reincarnation: The Phoenix Fire Mystery* (Julian Press/Crown, 1977) p. xvi.
5. G. Feinberg, *What is the World Made of?* (Anchor Press/Doubleday, 1977), cf. p. 31 and chapter 4.
6. The standard example usually cited as an illustration of this sort of scientific advance is that of the replacement of Newtonian by Einsteinian gravitation theory.
7. G. Murphy, *The Challenge of Psychical Research*, p. 273.

8. M. Poll, 'Religion in Britain', *Now!* (21 December 1979) p. 23.

9. Broad suggests that every conscious living creature may be a 'compound' of a bodily factor and a psychic factor which may survive bodily death, perhaps to be reincarnated in a new body or to 'possess' some already 'occupied' body. Cf. *The Mind and its Place in Nature* (RKP, 1949 (1925)) pp. 535–551, 651–3; *Lectures on Psychical Research*, pp. 387ff.

10. J. Hick, *Death and Eternal Life* (Collins, 1976) p. 378.

11. When working in parishes as a priest I was constantly struck by how often the *de facto* ground for belief in life after death was confidence in an apparitional appearance of this type. See also K. Osis and E. Haraldsson, *At the Hour of Death* (Avon, 1977) pp. 13–14.

12. Cf. 1 Corinthians 15.5–8 and discussion of 'ophthe' on p. 22 above. See also P. Badham, *Christian Beliefs about Life after Death* (Macmillan, 1976) chapter 2, for a fuller defence of this interpretation.

13. Acts 1.3.

14. Broad, *Lectures on Psychical Research*, p. 428. (I have inverted the order of the two phrases quoted.)

15. Hick, *Death and Eternal Life*, p. 142.

16. G. N. M. Tyrrell, *The Personality of Man* (Penguin, 1948) pp. 162–3.

17. An account of contemporary discussions of this theory may be found in my *Christian Beliefs*, chapter 9.

18. P. F. Strawson, *Individuals* (Methuen, 1959) p. 116.

19. Cf. E. L. Mascall, *Grace and Glory* (Faith Press, 1961).

20. St Thomas Aquinas, *Summa Contra Gentiles*, Bk. 3, pt. 1; cited by Hick, *Death and Eternal Life*, p. 206.

21. Augustine, *Confessions* 1.1, linked to a Compline prayer derived from Augustine.

22. On the other hand, the 'being of light' seemed to form an important part of the near-death experiences of even atheists who were resuscitated. This might suggest that the religious dimension could become immediately real in the life hereafter.

23. Cf. Hick, *Death and Eternal Life*, pp. 315ff. for Hindu thought and pp. 350 off. for Buddhist thought.

24. K. Heim, *Christian Faith and the Natural Sciences* (SCM, 1953).

25. For a defence of this see my *Christian Beliefs*, pp. 67–9, 90–3.

26. Cf. Hick, *Death and Eternal Life*, Part V.

27. For a defence of this see my *Christian Beliefs*, pp. 13–17. Note also that Schleiermacher was not against doctrine as such, but only against doctrinal formulations which do not arise out of living Christian experience. His own major work, *The Christian Faith* shows how full on account can be given of the faith in modern terms when experience is seen as the central foundation.

28. E. Schillebeeckx, *Christ, the Christian experience in the Modern World* (SCM, 1980), p. 797.

Select Bibliography

W. R. Alger, *The Destiny of the Soul* (1860; Greenwood Press, 1968).

Norman Autton, *The Pastoral Care of the Dying* (SPCK, 1966).

A. J. Ayer, *The Central Questions of Philosophy* (Penguin, 1976).

Paul Badham, *Christian Beliefs about Life after Death* (Macmillan, 1976; SPCK, 1978).

Susan Blackmore, *Parapsychology and out-of-the-body experiences* (Transpersonal Books, 1978).

C. D. Broad, *Lectures on Psychical Research* (RKP, 1962).

R. Bultmann, 'New Testament and Mythology', in H. W. Bartsch *Kerygma and Myth* (Harper, 1961).

Sir Cyril Burt, *Psychology and Psychical Research* (Society for Psychical Research, 1968).

P. Dearmer, *The Legend of Hell* (Cassell, 1929).

D. L. Edwards, *The Last Things Now* (SCM, 1969).

Antony Flew, *Body, Mind and Death* (Macmillan, 1964).

Antony Flew, *The Presumption of Atheism* (Elek, 1976).

Jonathan Glover, *Causing Death and Saving Lives* (Penguin, 1977).

J. C. Hampe, *To Die is Gain* (DLT, 1979).

John Hick, *Death and Eternal Life* (Collins, 1976).

David Hume, *On Religion*, ed. R. Wollheim (Fontana, 1963).

J. Iverson, *More Lives than One?* (Pan, 1977).

Nicholas Lash, *Theology on Dover Beach* (DLT, 1979).

Sir Bernard Lovell, 'Creation', in *Theology*, vol. LXXXIII, no. 695, September 1980.

John Macquarrie, *The Christian Hope* (Mowbrays, 1978).

E. L. Mascall, *Christian Theology and Natural Science* (Longmans, Green, 1956).

E. L. Mascall, *The Importance of Being Human* (OUP, 1959).

A. S. Mason, *Health and Hormones* (Penguin, 1960).

Mary Midgley, *Beast and Man* (Methuen, 1979).

E. D. Mitchell, *Psychic Exploration* (Putnam, 1974).

J. Moltmann, *The Crucified God* (SCM, 1973).

J. Moltmann, *Theology of Hope* (SCM, 1967).

R. A. Moody, *Life after Life* (Bantam, 1977).

R. A. Moody, *Reflections on Life after Life* (Corgi, 1978).

V. H. Mottram, *The Physical Basis of Personality* (Penguin, 1944).

G. Murphy, *The Challenge of Psychical Research* (Harper, 1961).

K. Osis and E. Haraldsson, *At the Hour of Death* (Avon, 1977).

K. Osis, *Deathbed Observations of Physicians and Nurses* (Parapsychology Foundation, 1961).

T. Penelhum, *Survival and Disembodied Existence* (RKP, 1970).

D. Z. Phillips, *Death and Immortality* (Macmillan, 1970).

Norman Pittenger, *After Death, Life in God* (SCM, 1980).

K. R. Popper and J. C. Eccles, *The Self and its Brain* (Springer International, 1977).

H. J. Richards, *Death and After* (Fount, 1980).

E. Kubler Ross, 'Death does not exist', *Coevolution Quarterly*, (Summer 1977).

F. H. Saltmarsh, *The Evidence of Personal Survival from Cross-correspondences* (Bell, 1938).

A. Smith, *The Body* (Penguin, 1978).

J. R. Smythies, *Brain and Mind* (RKP, 1965).

Ian Stevenson, *Twenty Cases Suggestive of Reincarnation* (ASPR, 1966).

A. Toynbee, *Man's Concern with Death*, (Hodder, 1968).

S. Travis, *Christian Hope and the Future of Man* (Inter-Varsity Press, 1980).

G. N. M. Tyrrell, *The Personality of Man* (Penguin, 1948).

M. de Unamuno, *The Tragic Sense of Life* (Macmillan, 1912; Fontana, 1967).

B. Williams, *Problems of the Self* (CUP, 1973).

H. A. Williams, *True Resurrection* (Mitchell Beazley, 1972).

Index

Kornfield, D. S., 73
Kurtz, P., 72

Lampe, G. W. H., 25
Lancet, the, 71–2
Lash, N., 18, 20, 30, 51
Last Judgement, 32, 62
Leakey, R., 46
Lecky, W. E. H., 63
Lee, R. S., 43
Leggett, D. M. A., 74
Lippmann, W., 17
Litanies for the dead and dying, 29
Lombard, Peter, 51, 62
Lovell, Sir Bernard, 53, 55
Lowe, G., 45

McHarg, J., 81
Macquarrie, John, 6, 34–6
Mark, St, Gospel of, 23–4
Mary I, Queen of England, 63
Mascall, E. L., 52, 54, 56
Mead, M., 115
Mediumship, 93–8
Mill, J. S., 64
Mind-dependent World, 120–1
Mitchell, J. L., 78
Moltmann, J., 18, 20, 126
Moody, R. A., 71–8, 83
Moore, E. Garth, 74
Mottram, V. H., 40
Motyer, J. A., 64
Murphy, Gardner, 98, 113, 116
Myers, F. W. H., 95

Napoleon, 8–9
Newman, F. W., 61
Nicene Creed, 4, 67
Noyes, R., 82

Ogden, S., 16
Out-of-the-body experiences, 12–15, 71–8
Oppenheimer, H., 39
Osis, K., 76, 78, 92

Paul, St, 18–23, 25–6, 30
Personal Identity, 1–15

Personality, physiological basis of, 39–46
Peter, First Epistle of, 22–4
Peters, R. S., 60
Phillips, D. Z., 27–30
Pierce, C. S., 34
Pittenger, N., 32–5
Possession, 108–9, 118
Price, G. R., 90
Process theologians, 31–6
Puccetti, R., 56
Purgatory, 60, 133

Qumran covenanters, 26

Rahner, K., 34
Rawlings, M., 84–5
Reincarnation, 99–109, 117–18, 139
Requiem Mass, 14, 31
Resurrection, 4–6, 17–27, 36, 122
Richards, H. J., 18, 20
Rose, S., 43
Ross, E. K., 72, 74, 78, 80–1
Russell, B., 63

Sabom, M., 74
Sagan, C., 44, 53
Salter, W. H., 98
Schillebeeckx, E., 123
Schleiermacher, F., 58, 122
Shiels, D., 85
Simpson, M. A., 72, 82–3
Smith, A., 43
Smith, T., 80
Soul, 6, 10, 28–30, 36, 42, 89, 128
Spraggett, A., 81
Stepanek, P., 91
Stevenson, I., 99–102, 104–9
Storr, A., 106
Strawson, Sir Peter, 120

Tart, C., 76
Tertullian, 62
Thomas de Celano, 32
Thorpe, W. H., 49
Thouless, R. H., 15, 92
Tillich, P., 30
Turin Shroud, 127
Tyrrell, G. N. M., 92, 96, 119